AF574387

Oskar Schmidt
THE AMERICAN SERIES

Herausgeber / Editor
Matthias Harder

Oskar Schmidt

THE AMERI-CAN SERIES

DISTANZ

Ladder
2011

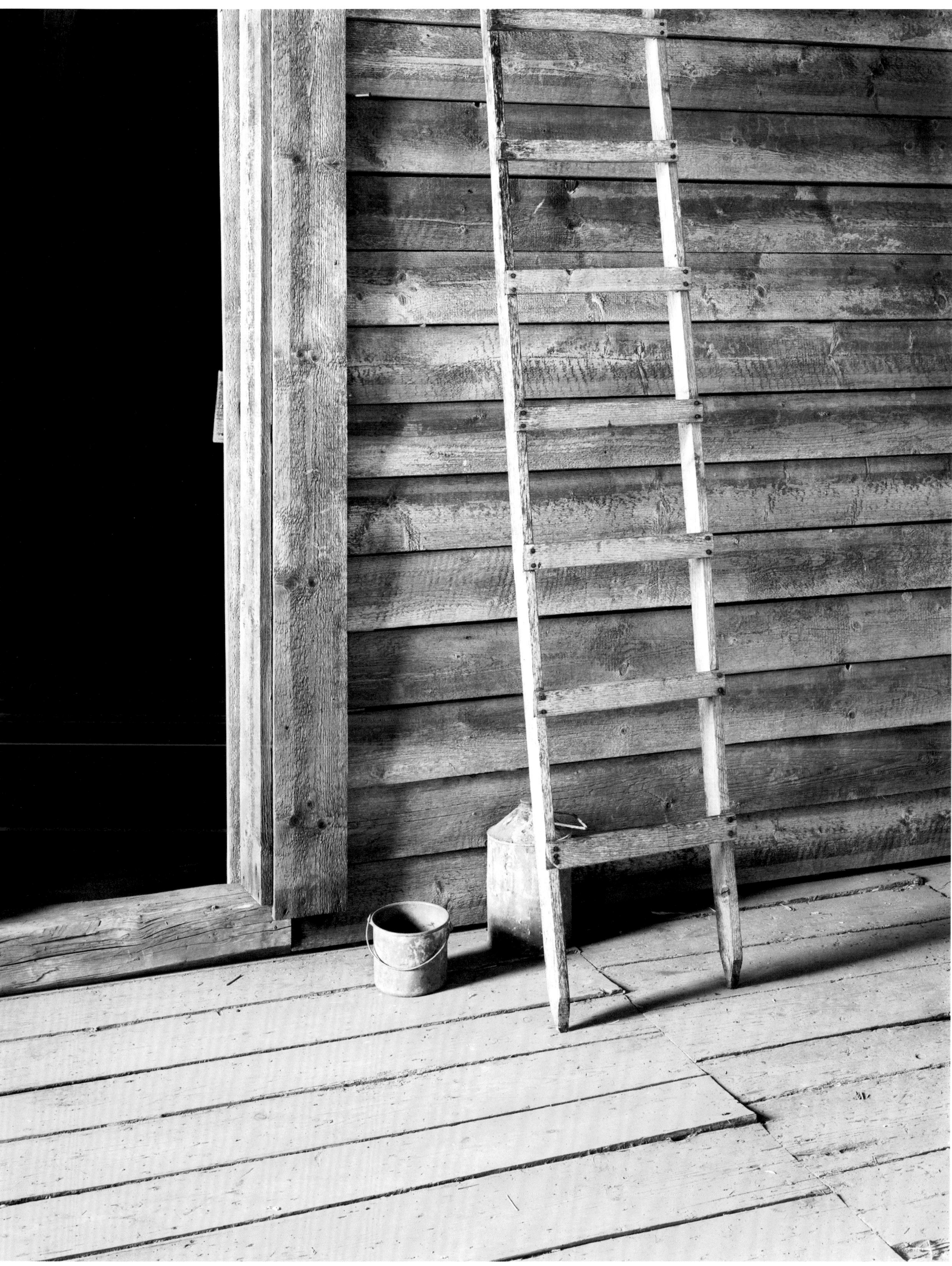

Cookware and Paper Bag
2011

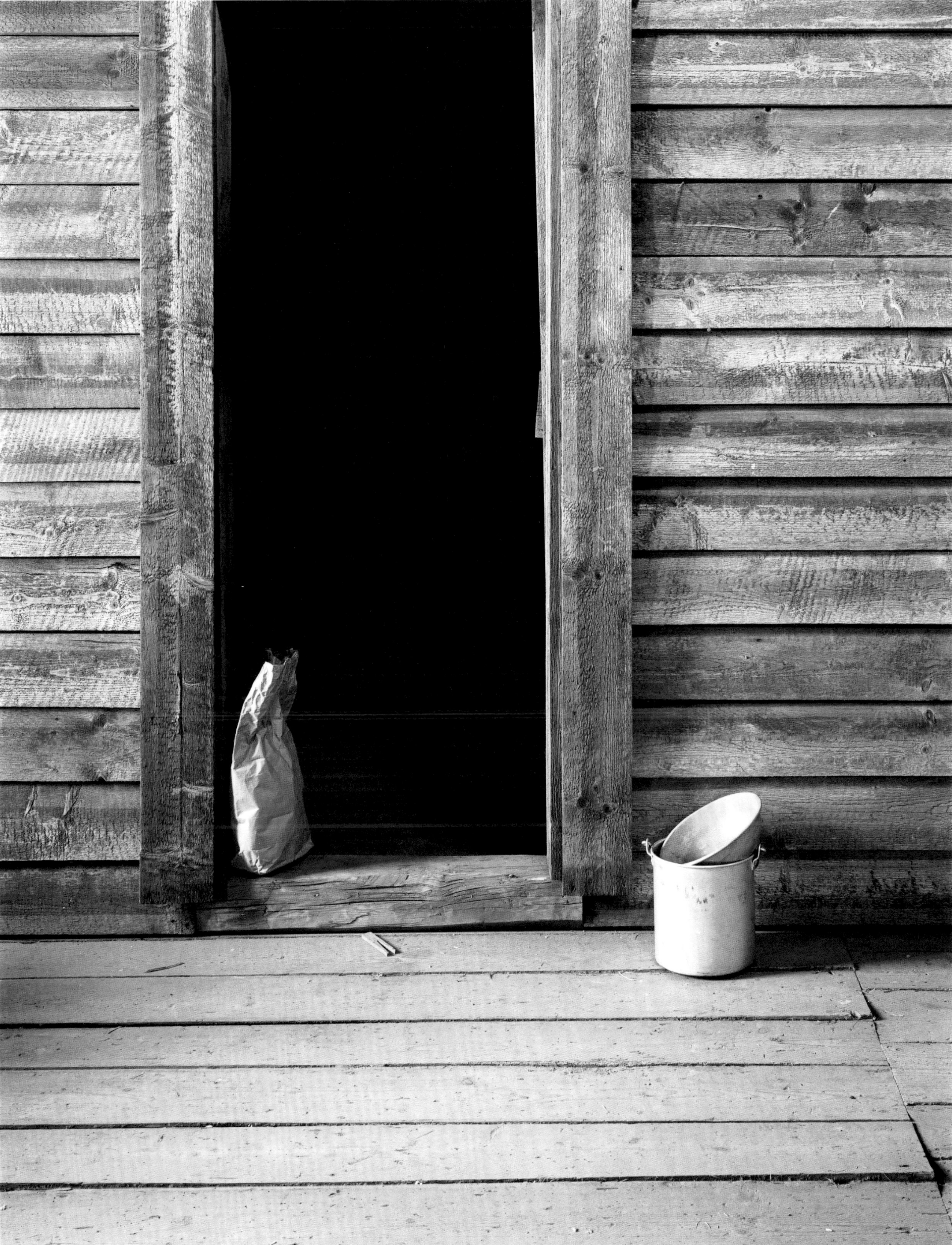

Oil Can and Towel
2011

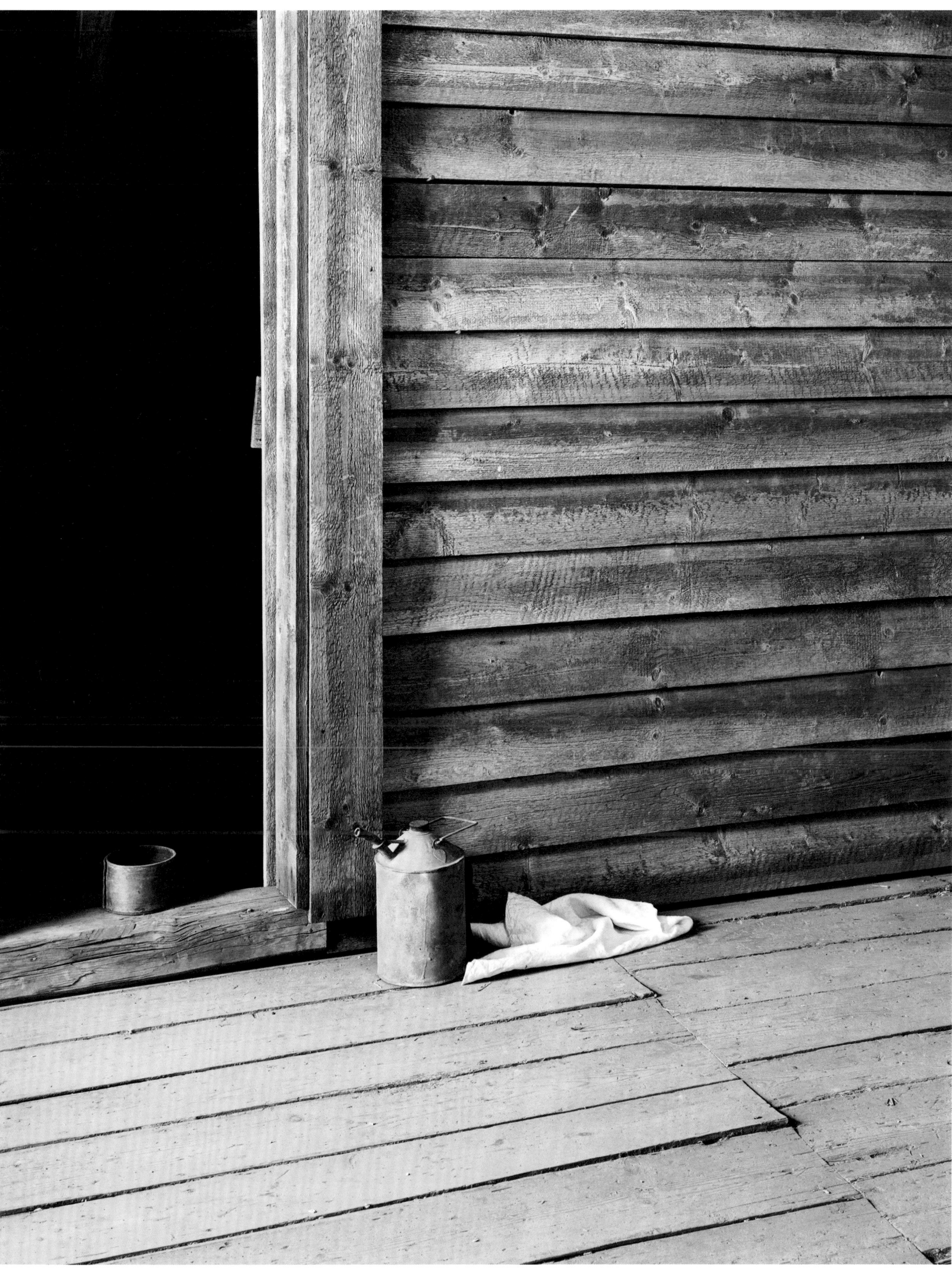

Dishes and Paper Bag
2012

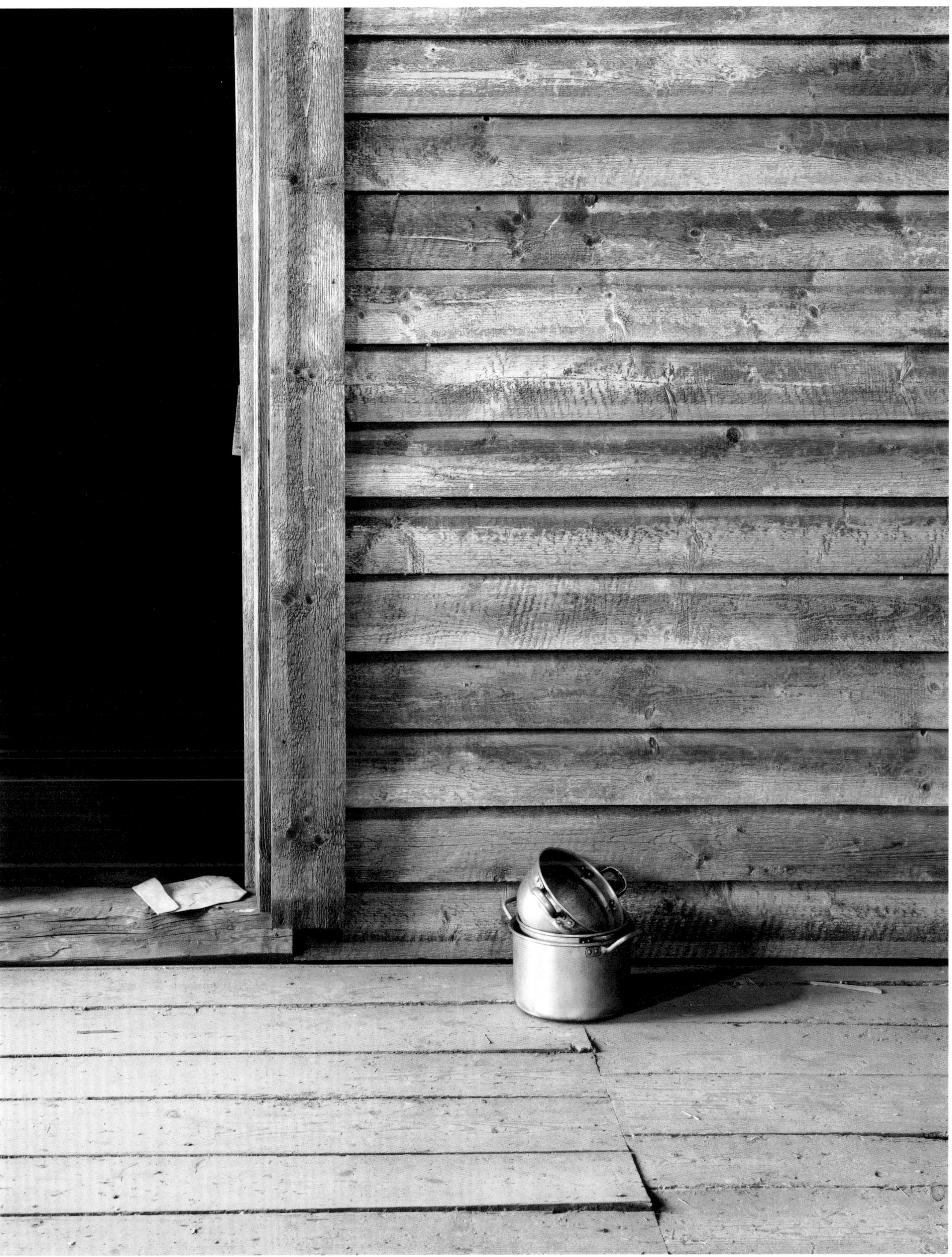

Kitchen Wall
2011

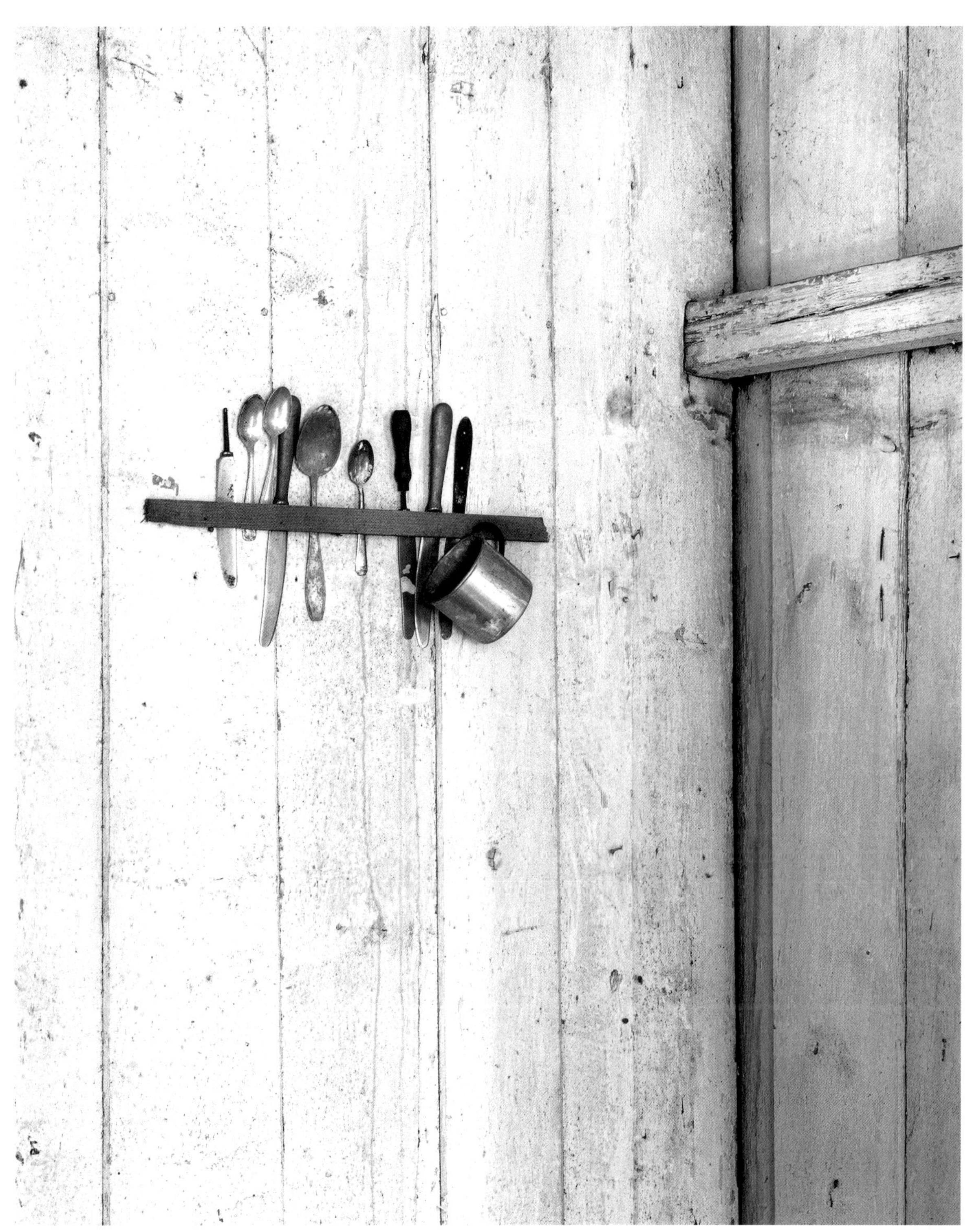

Cookware and Towel
2011

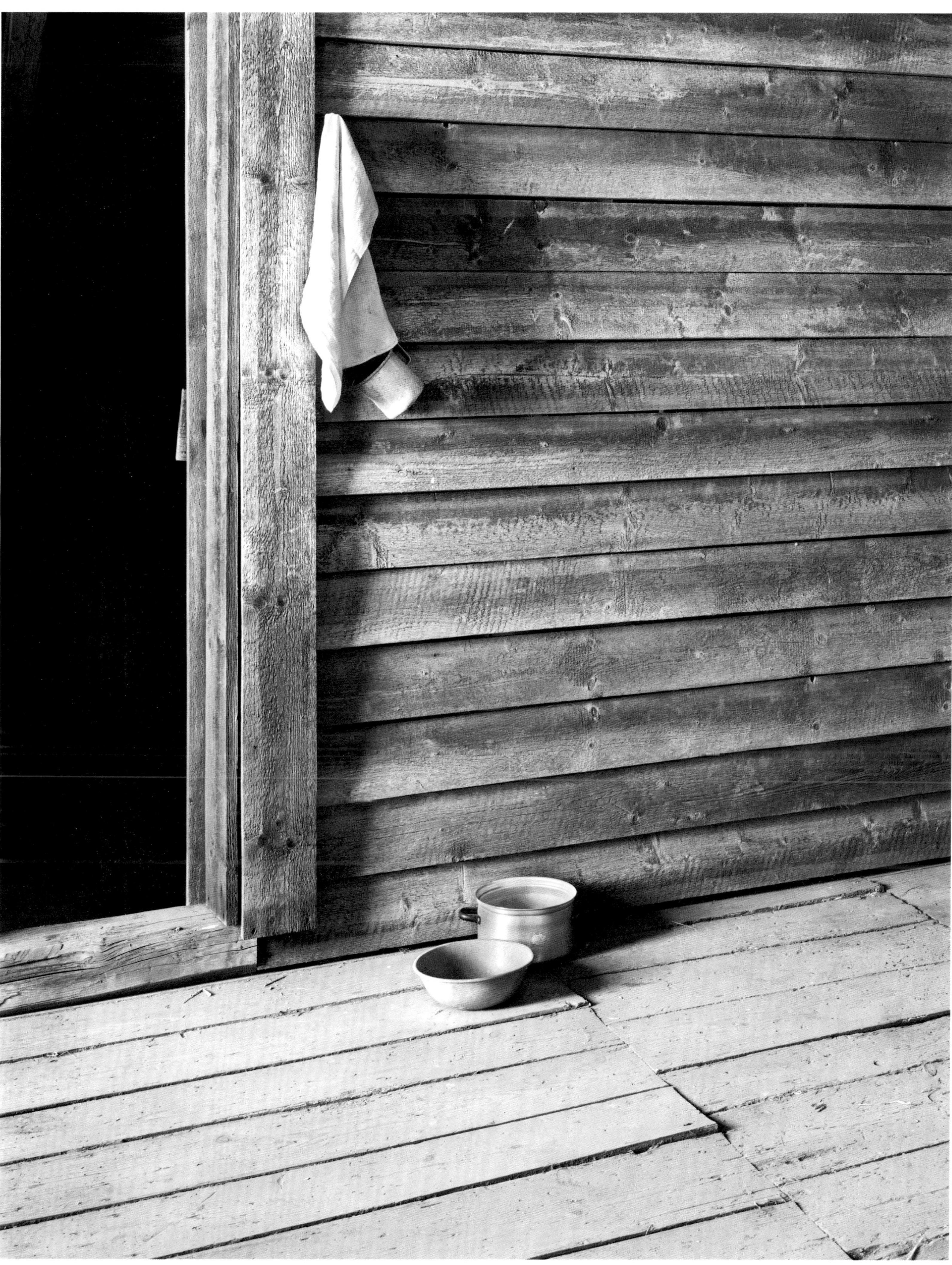

Jerry Can and Bottle
2011

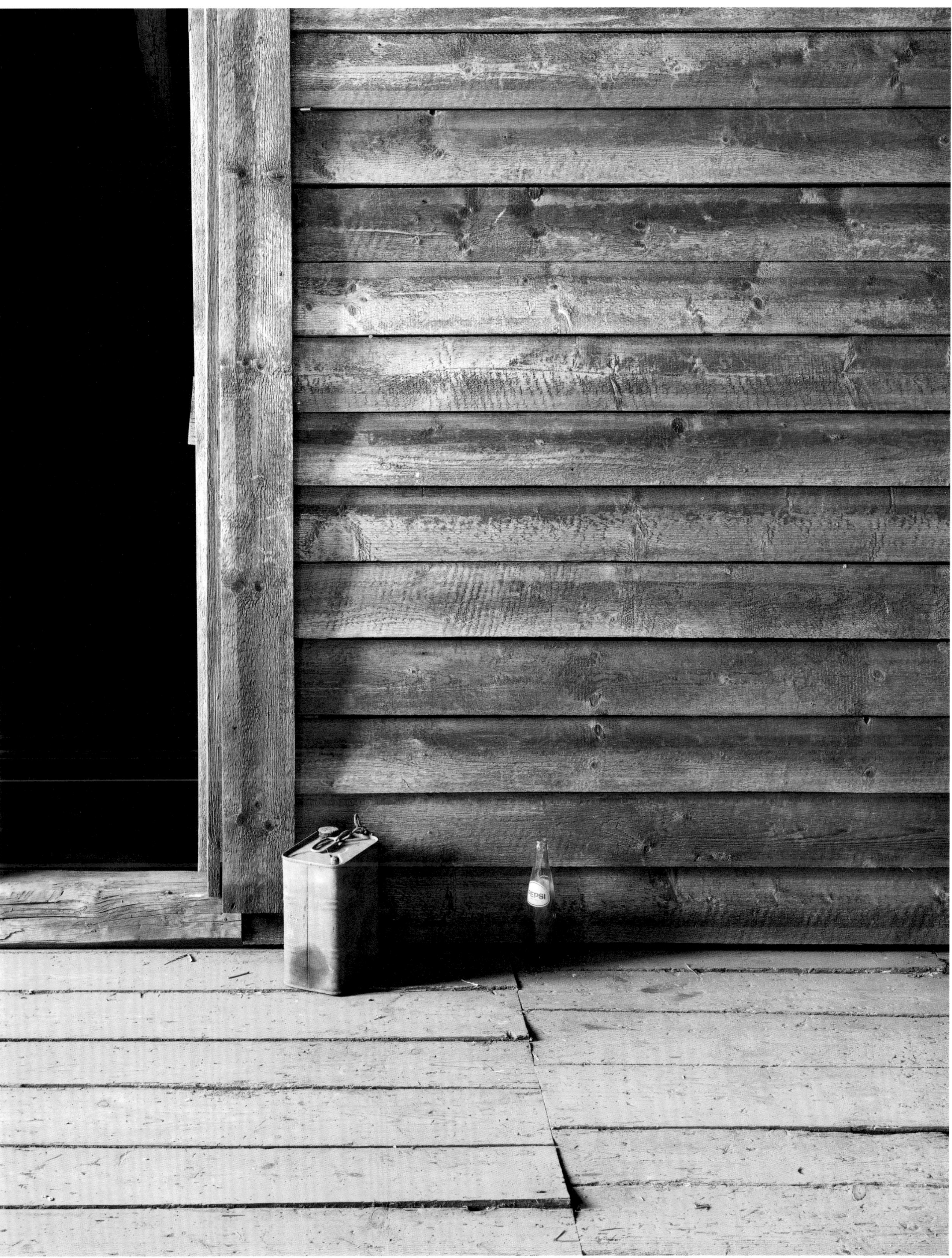
PEPSI

Bottle, Flatware and Pitcher
2011

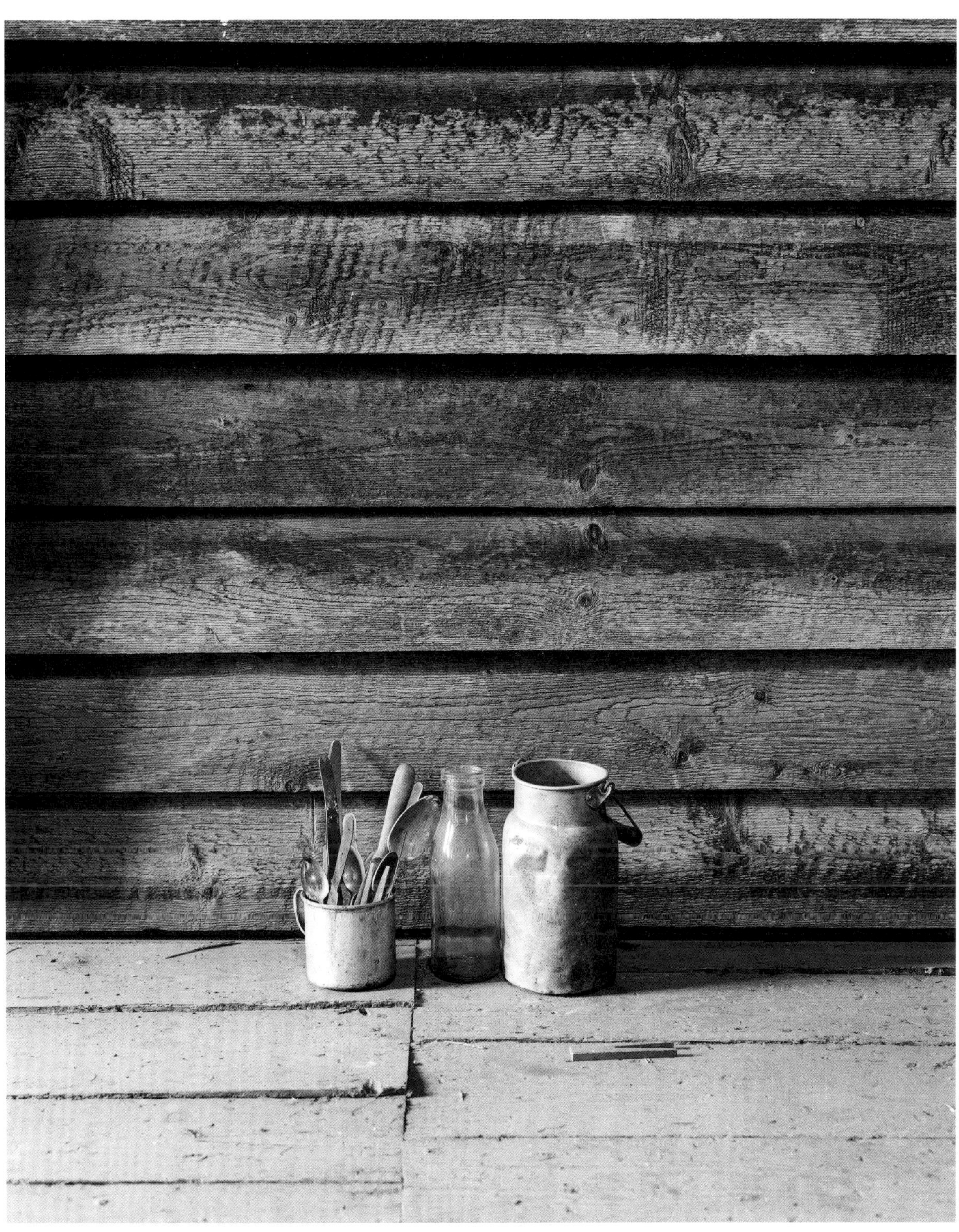

Metal Cans
2011

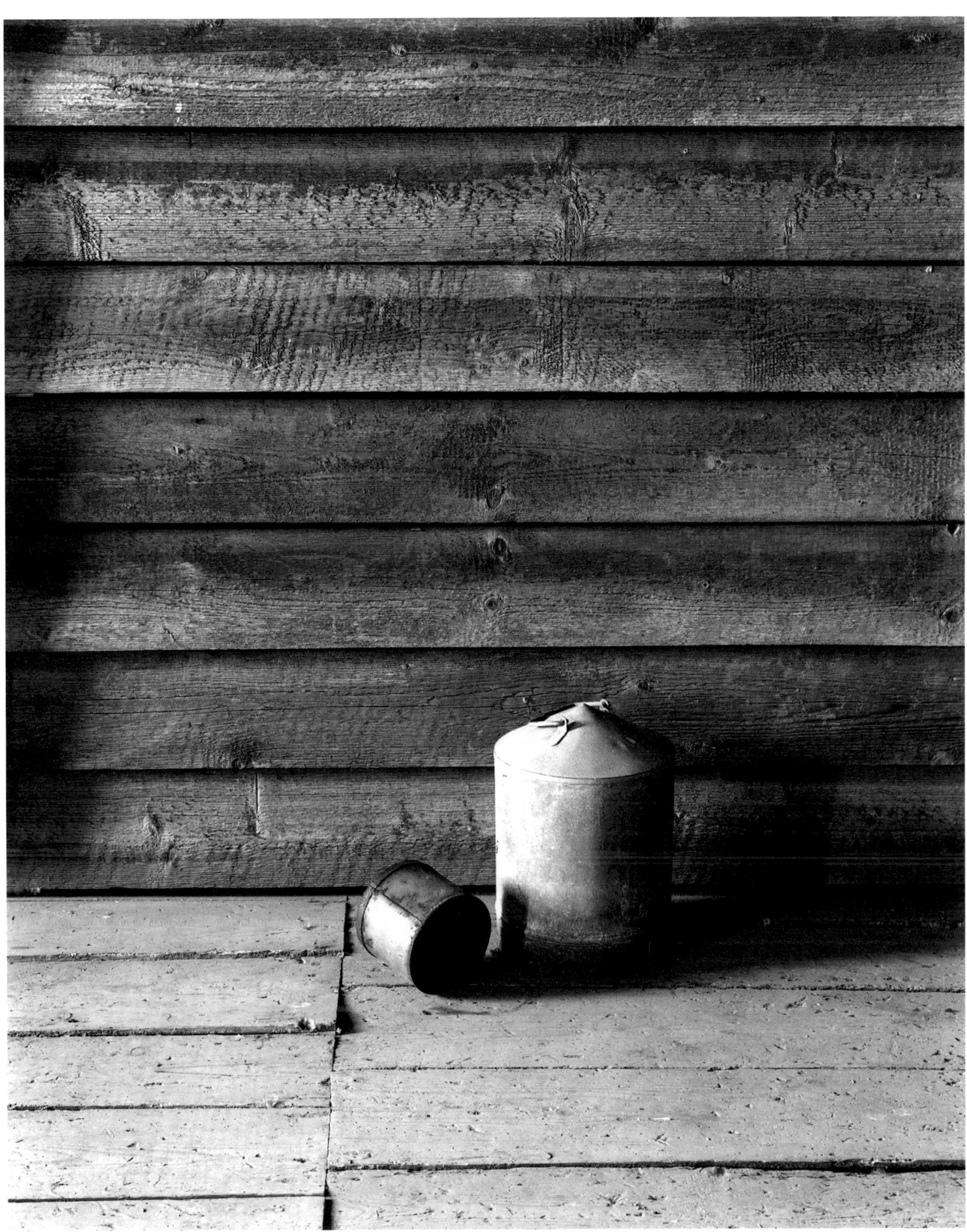

Chair
2011

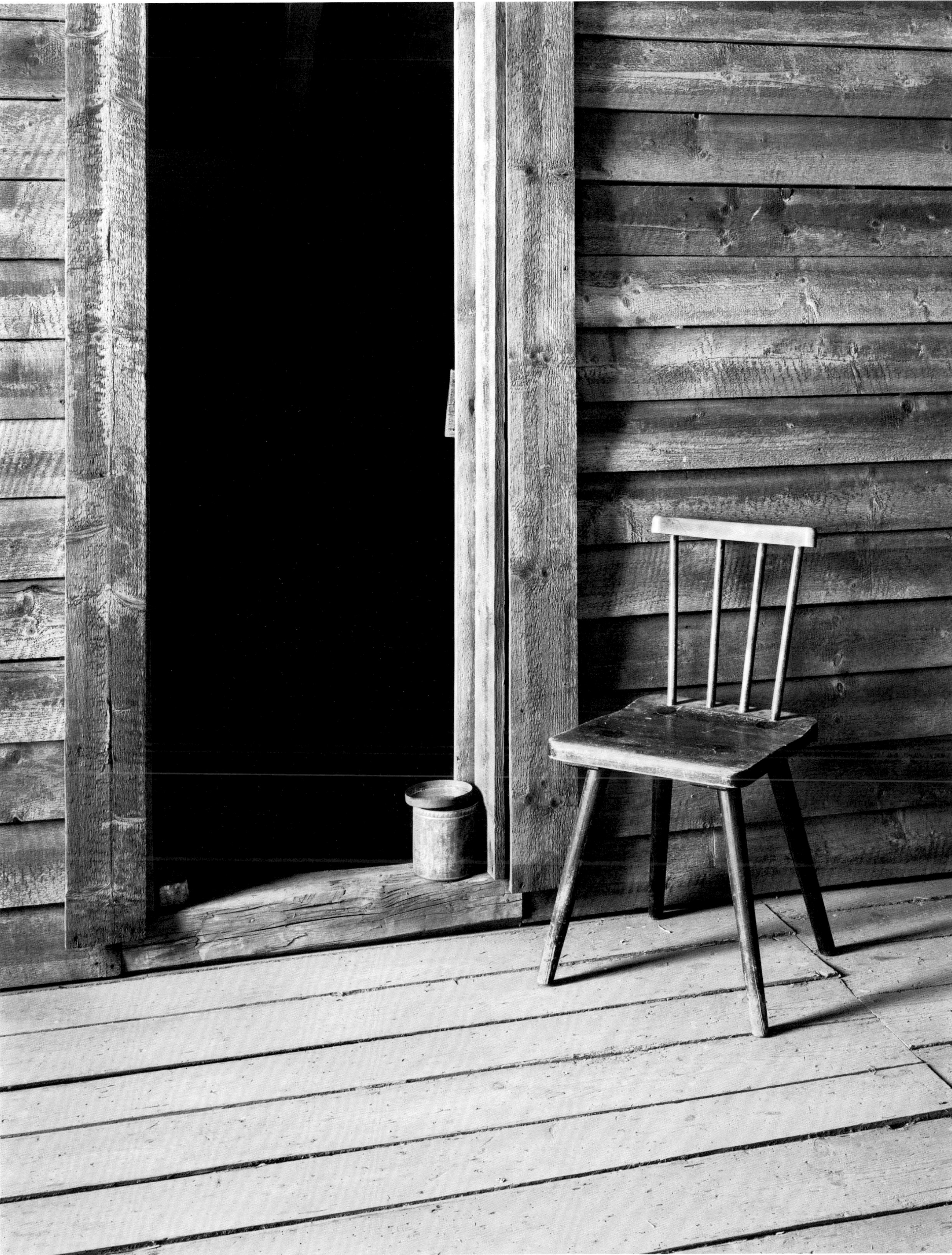

Bowl, Paper Bag and Pot
2012

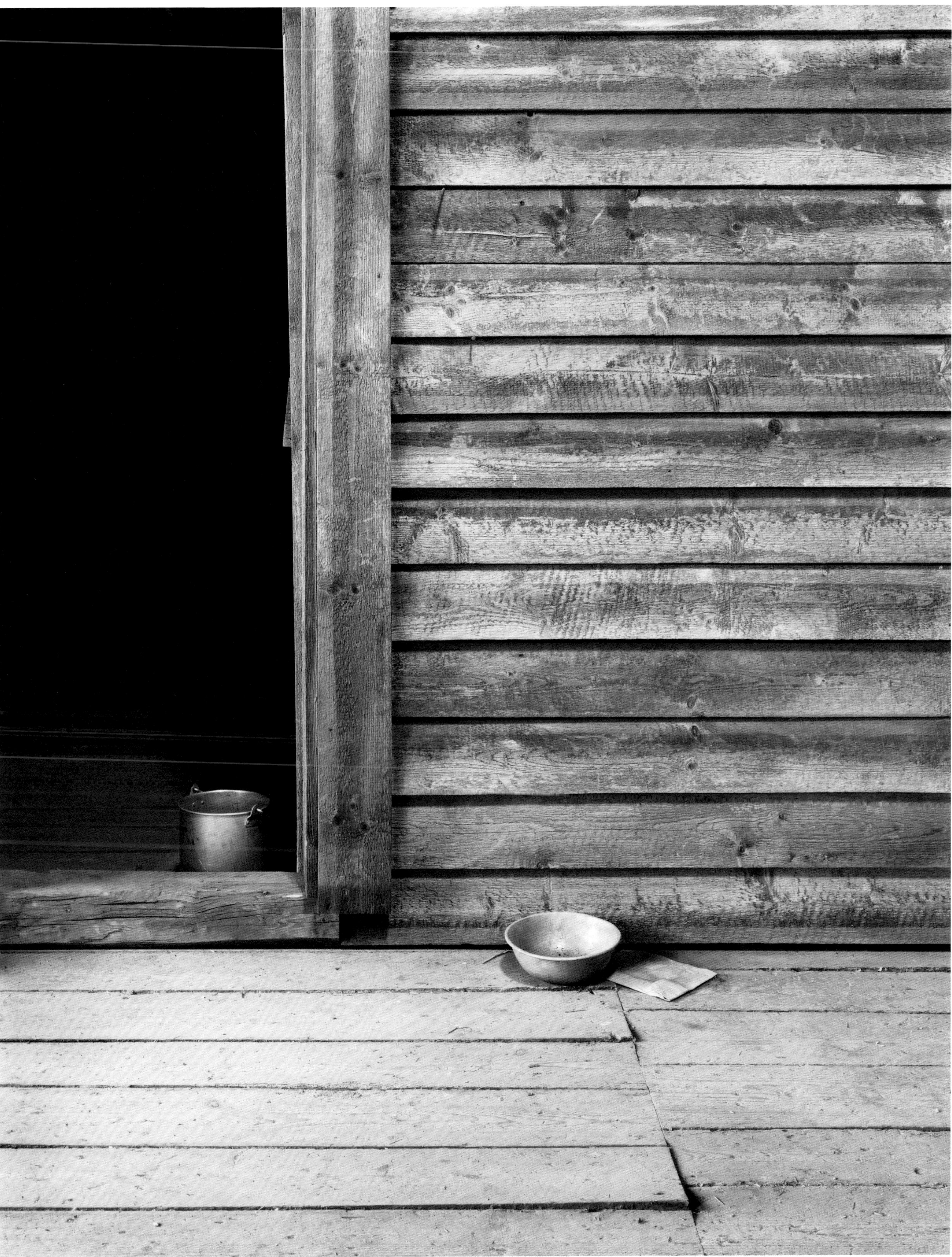

Mirrors and Metal Cup
2012

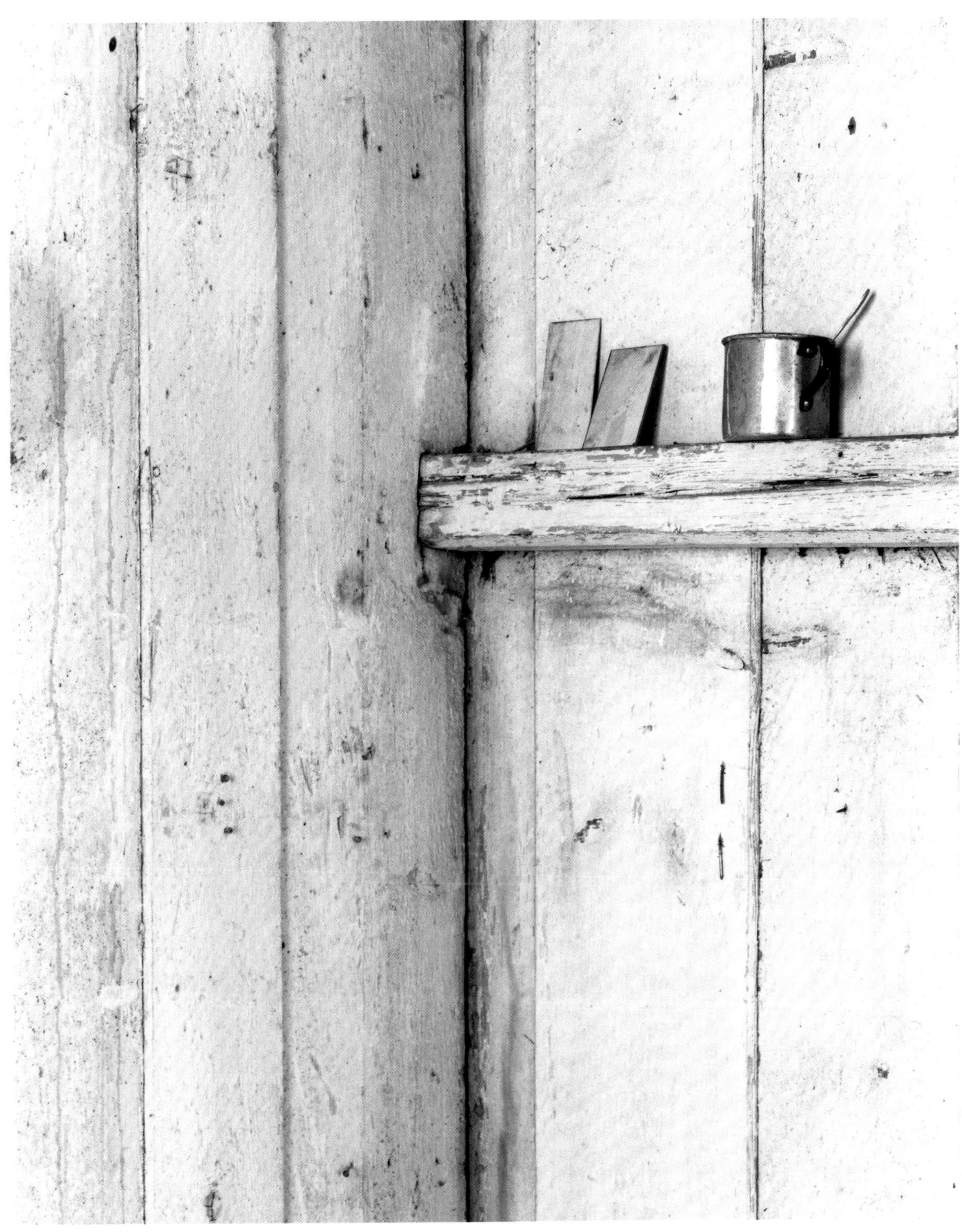

Can and Rope
2011

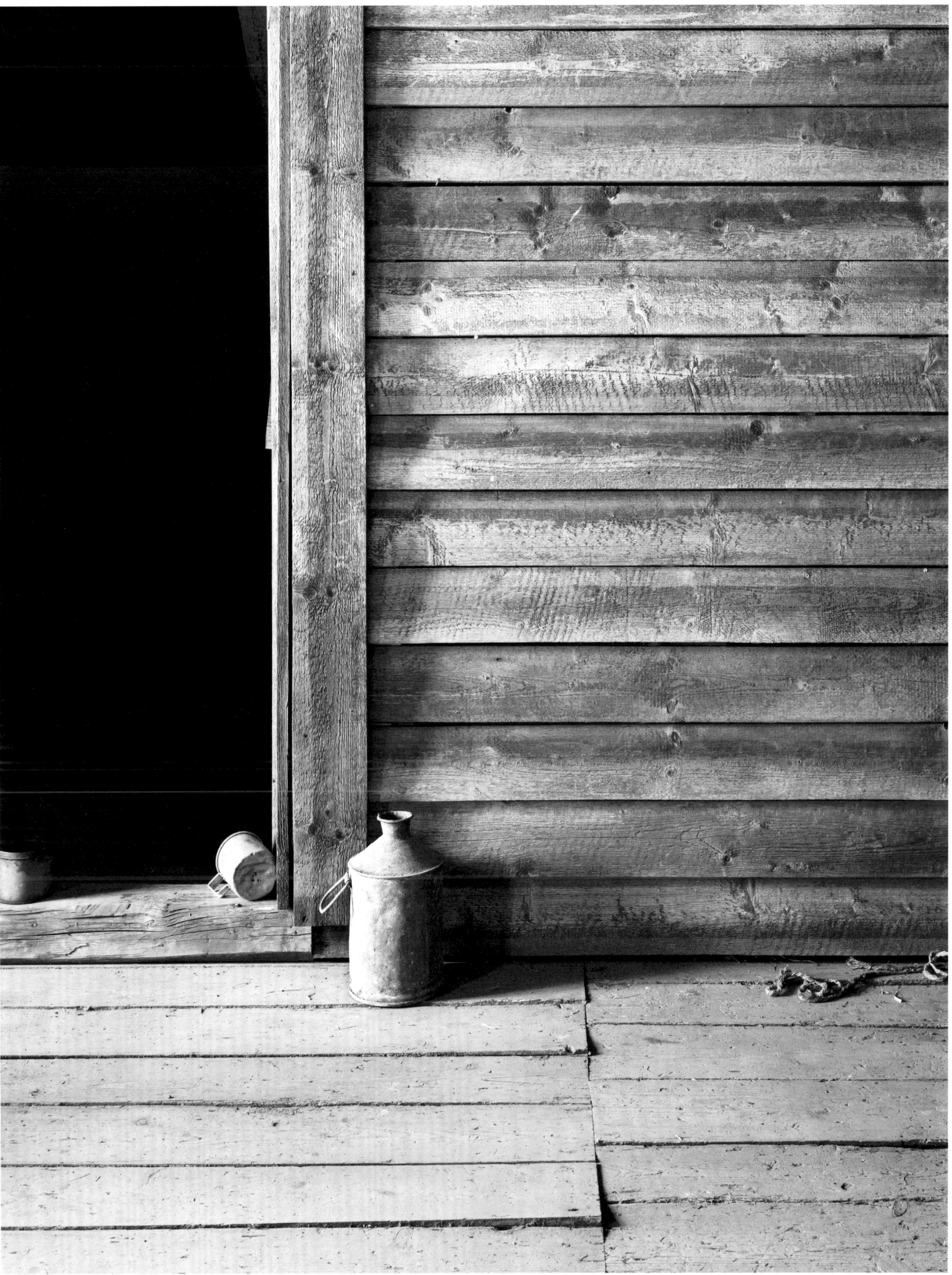

Lid and Bowls
2012

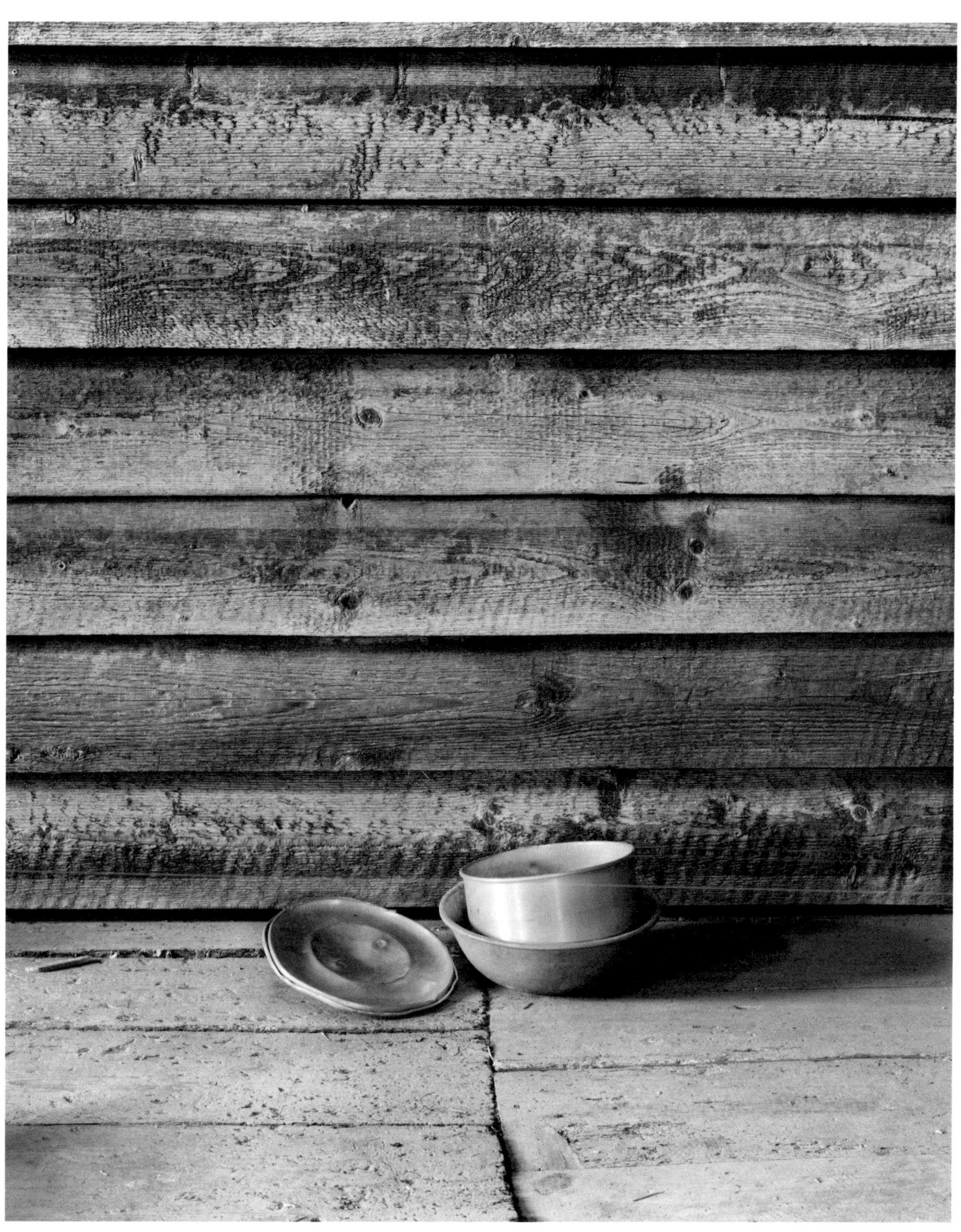

Metal Can and Paper Bag
2012

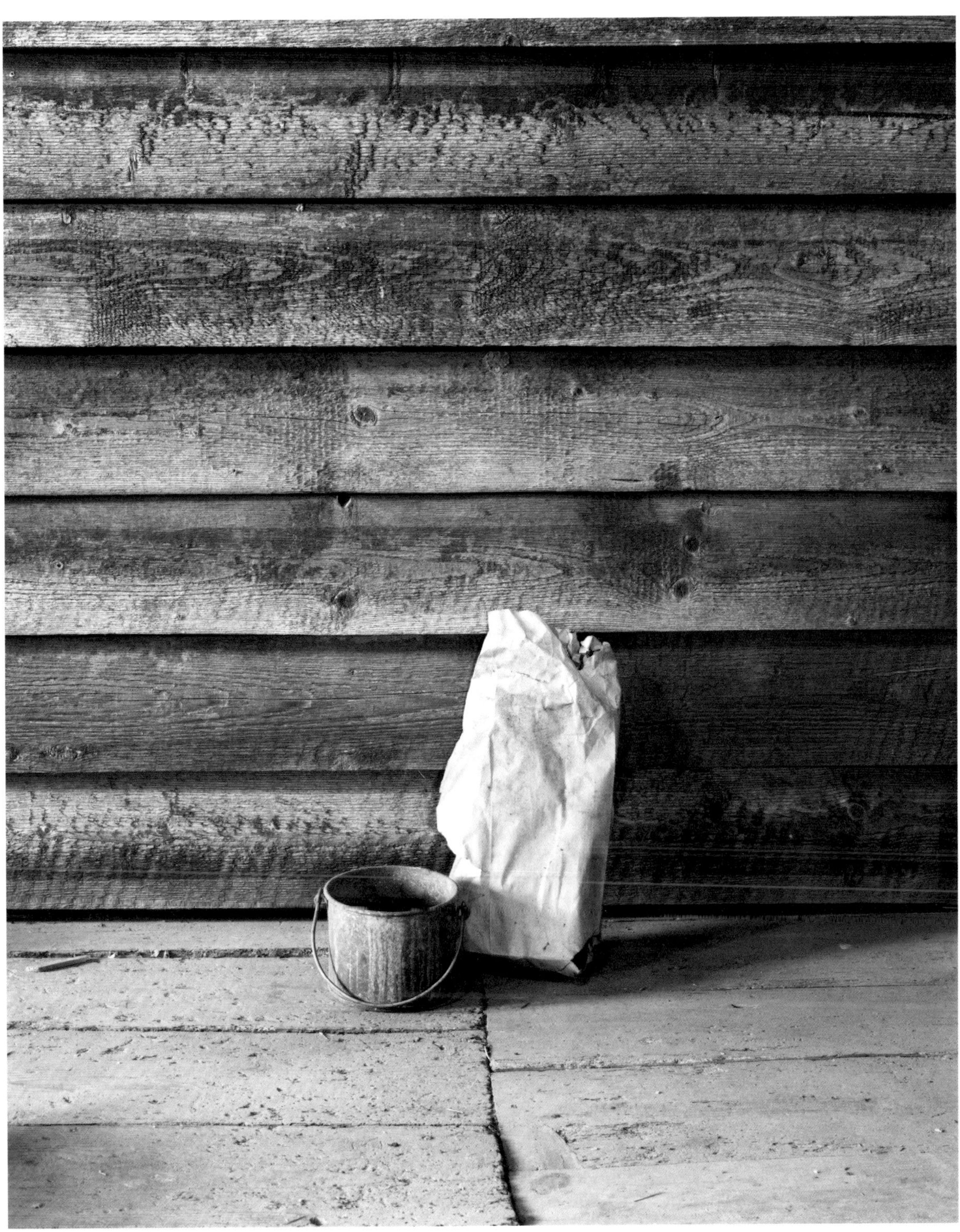

Two Cans
2011

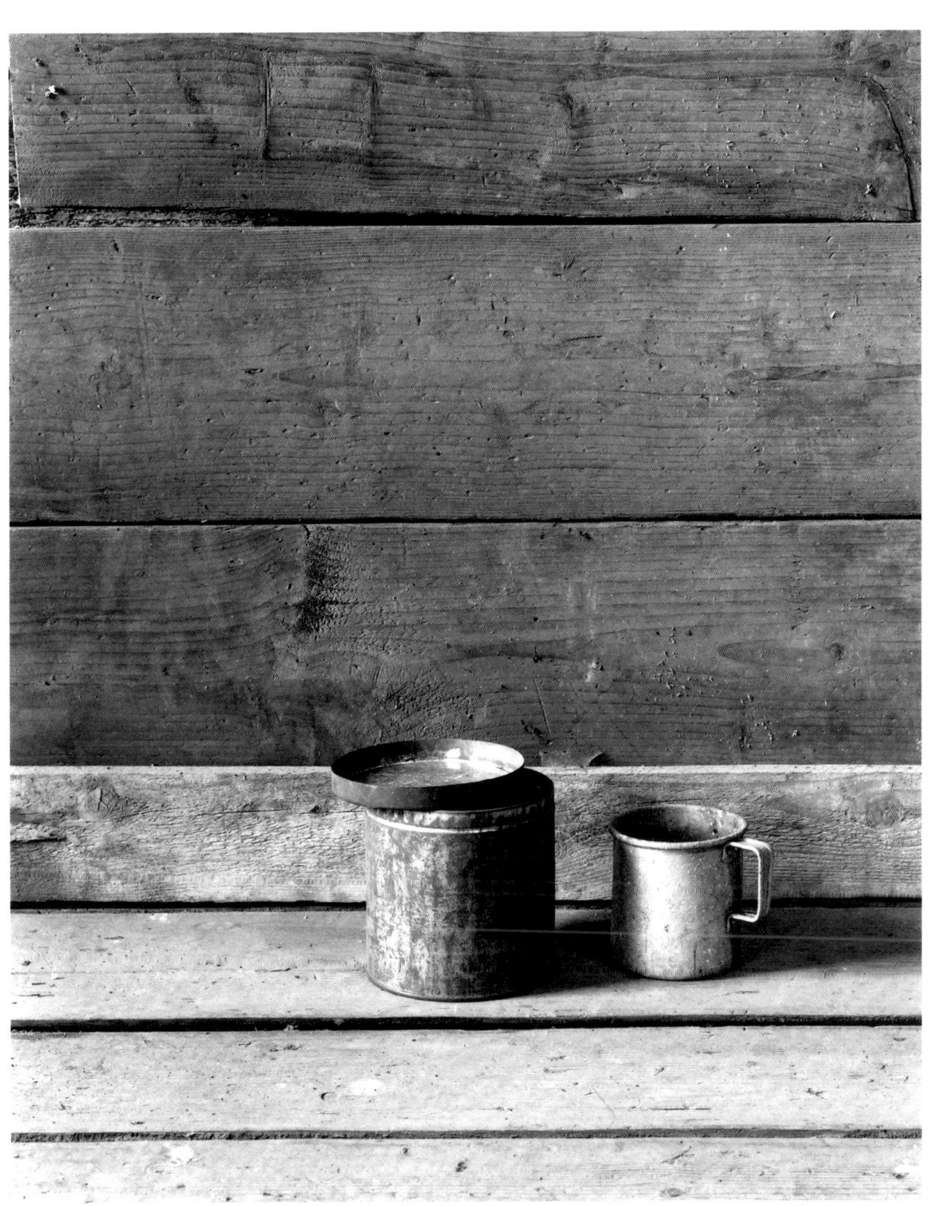

Dishes
2012

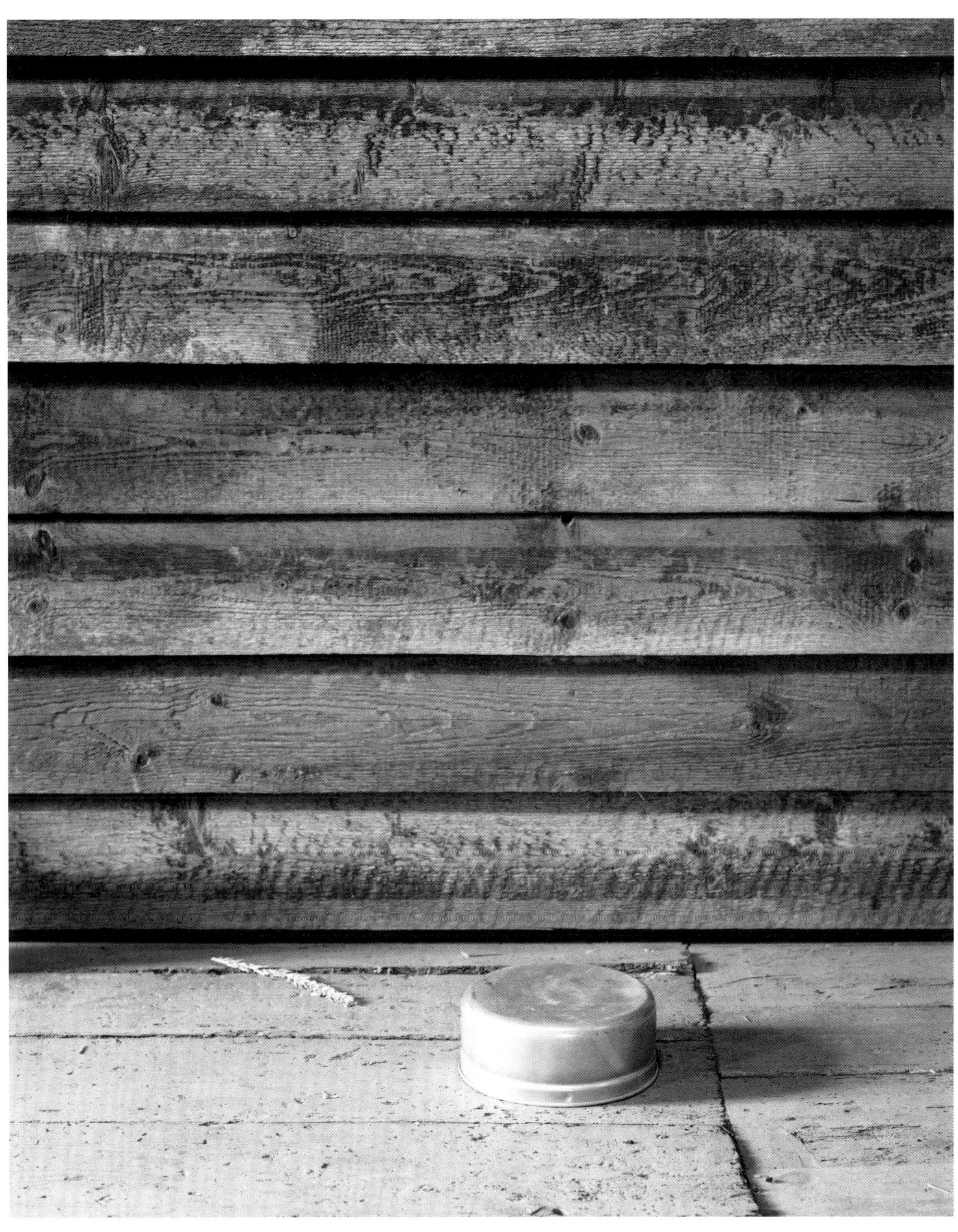

Paper Bag and Can
2012

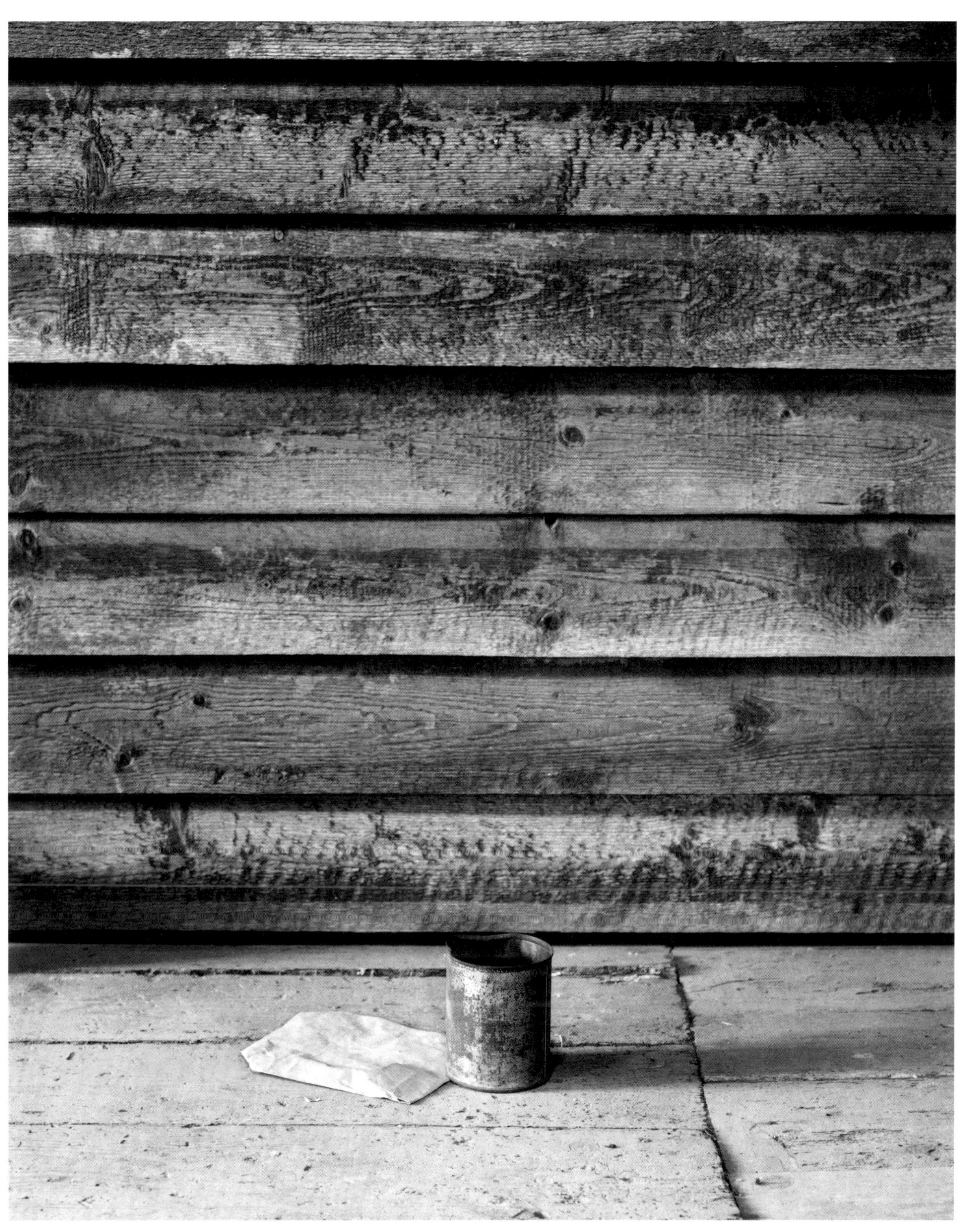

Bottle and Lid
2012

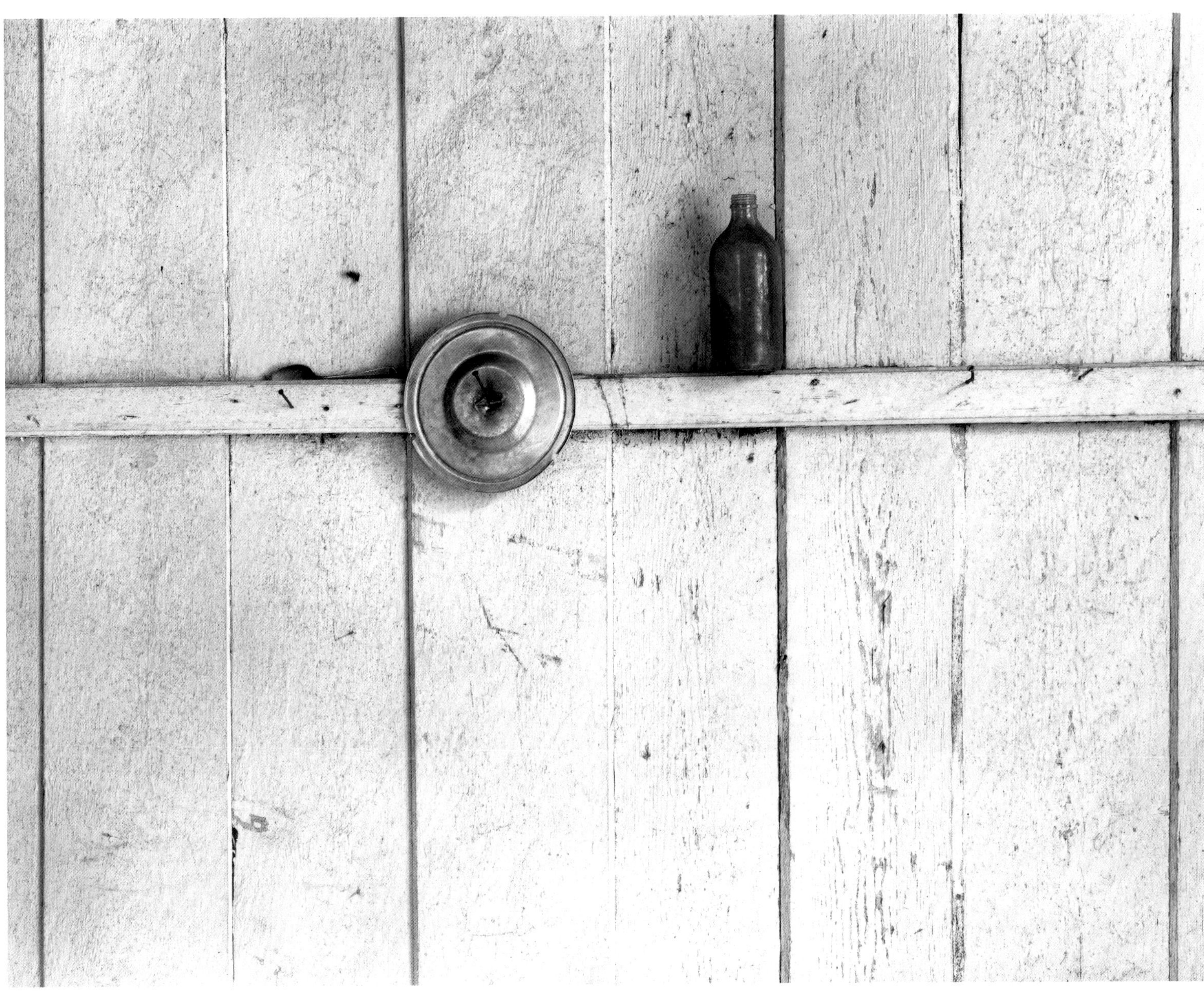

Bottle
2013

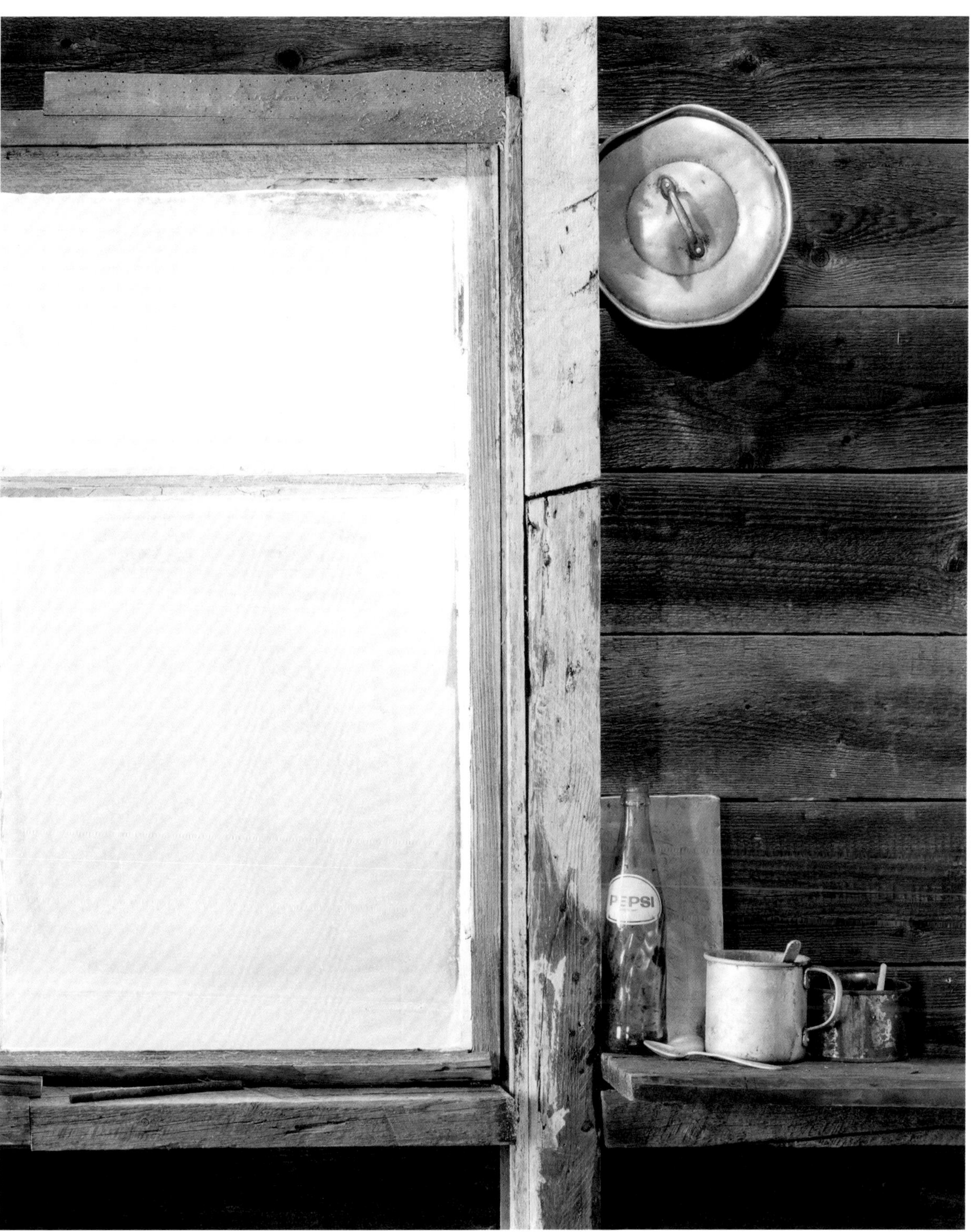
PEPSI

Picture
2013

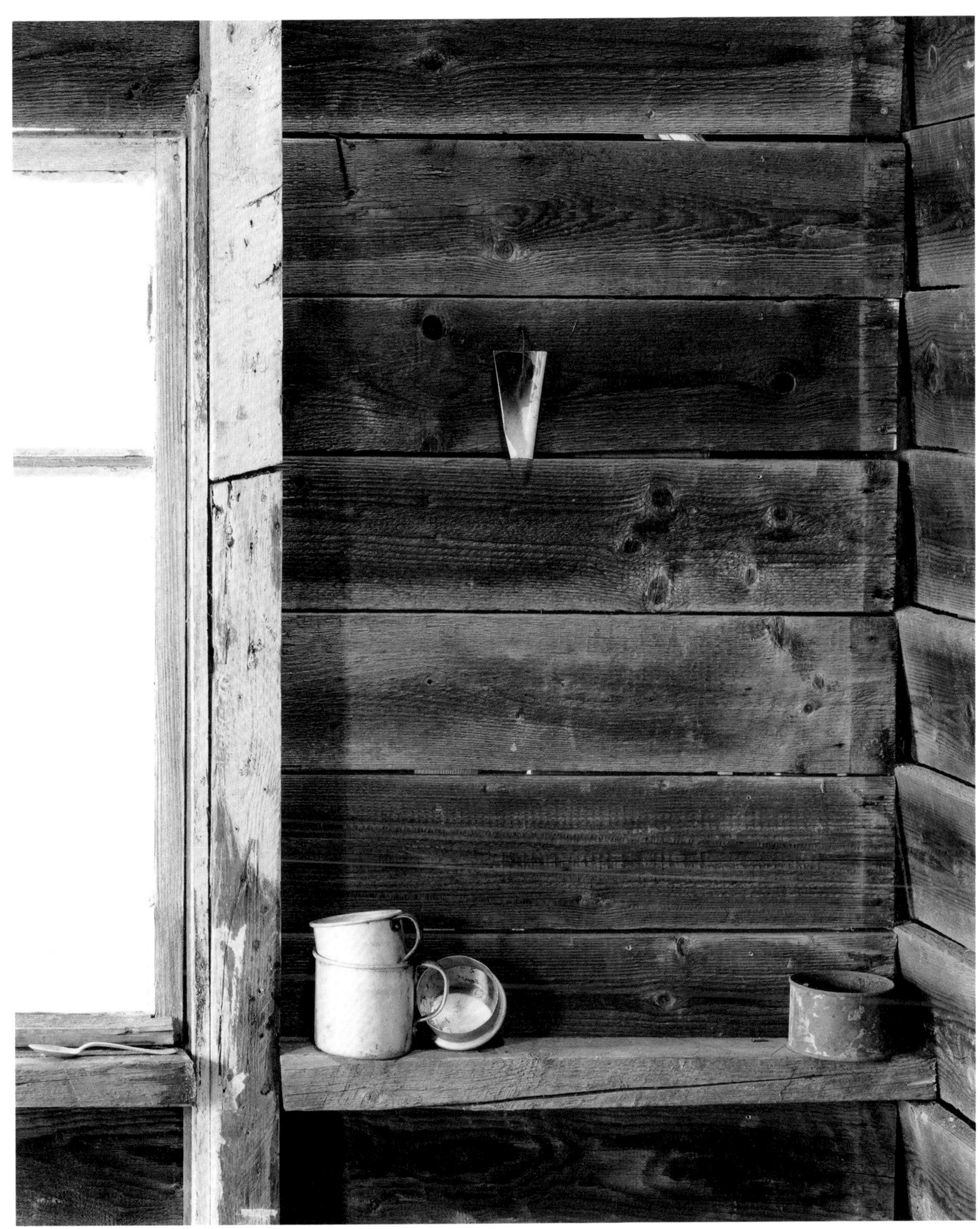

Tin
2013

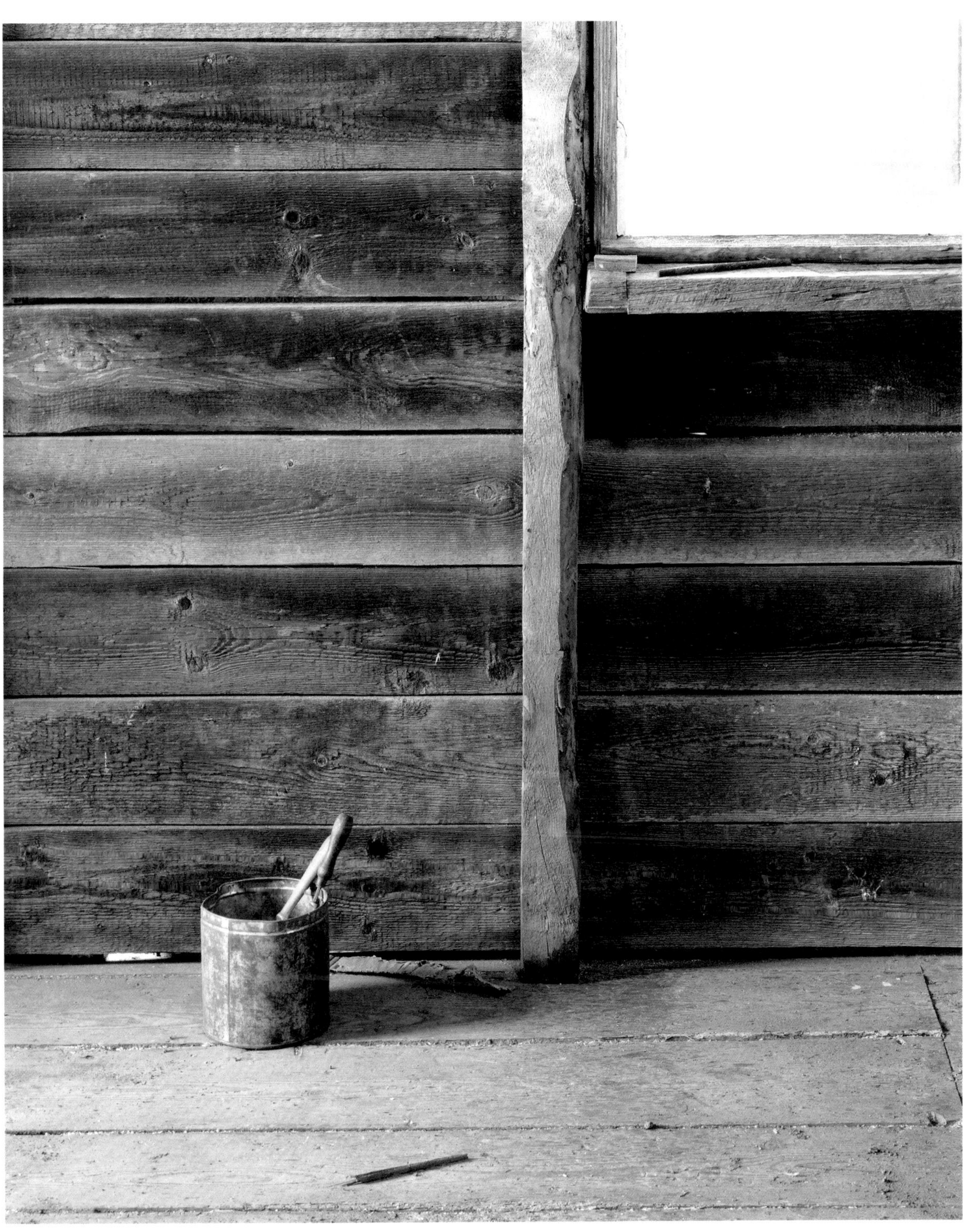

Metal Cup
2013

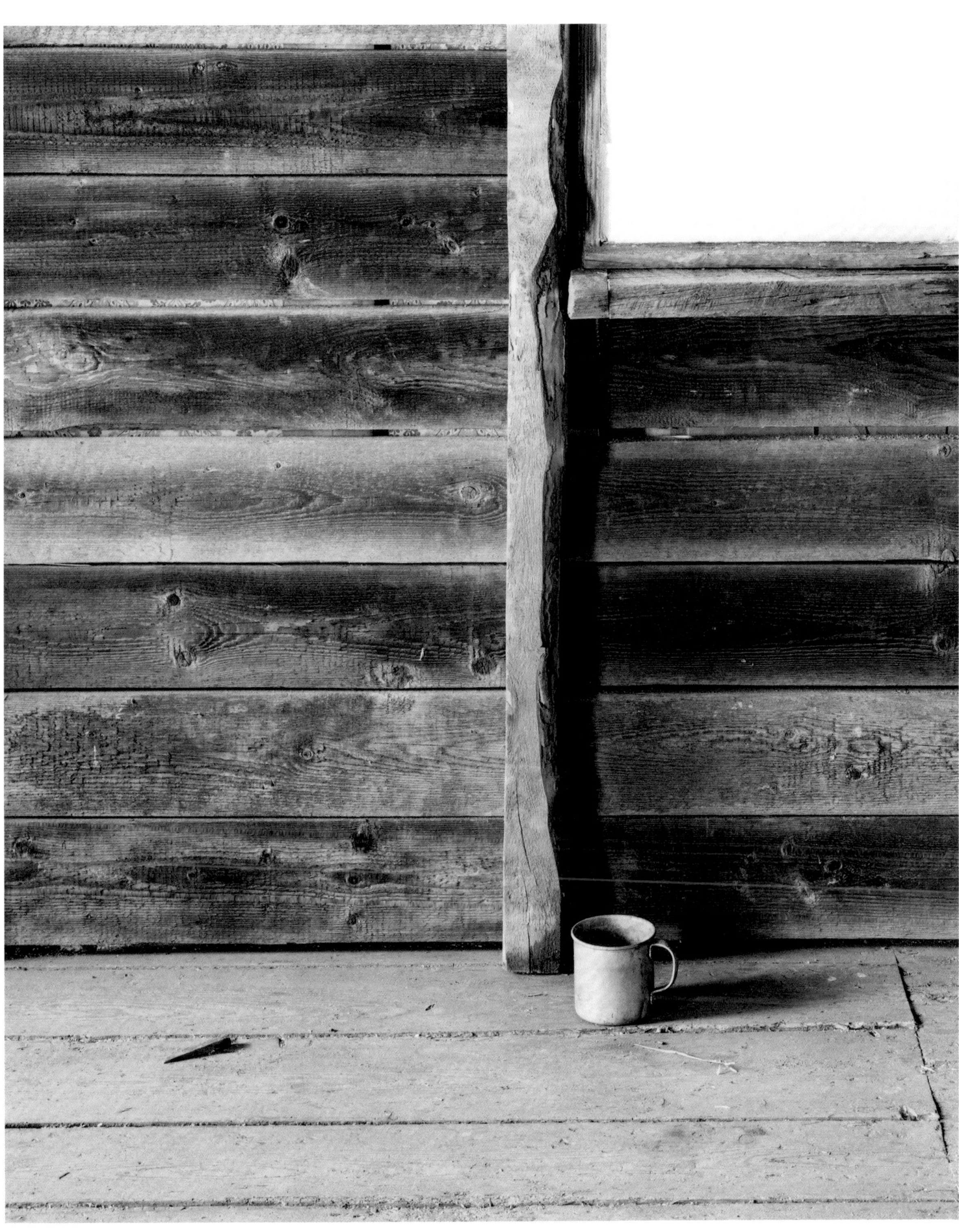

Mirror
2013

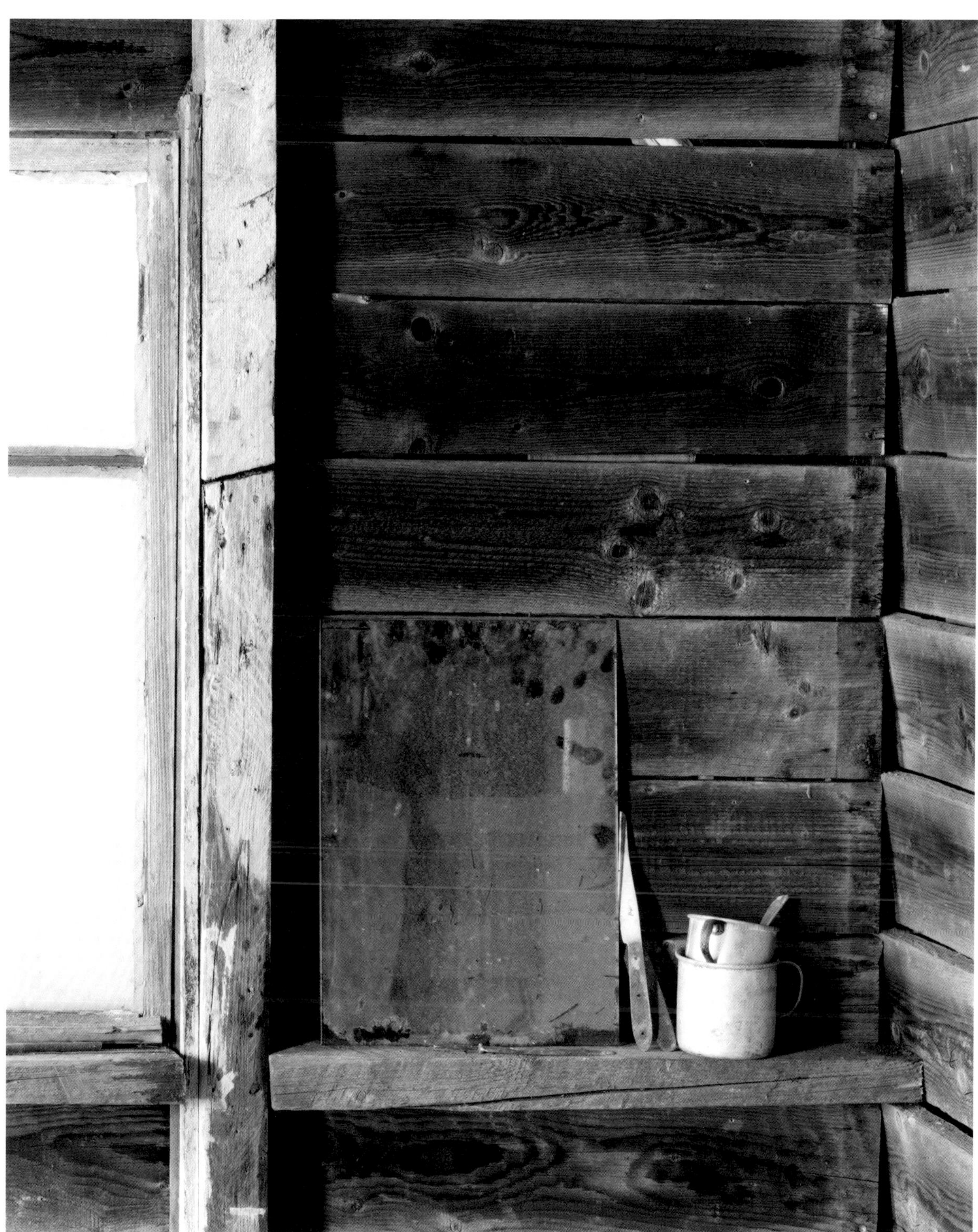

Metal Bowl
2013

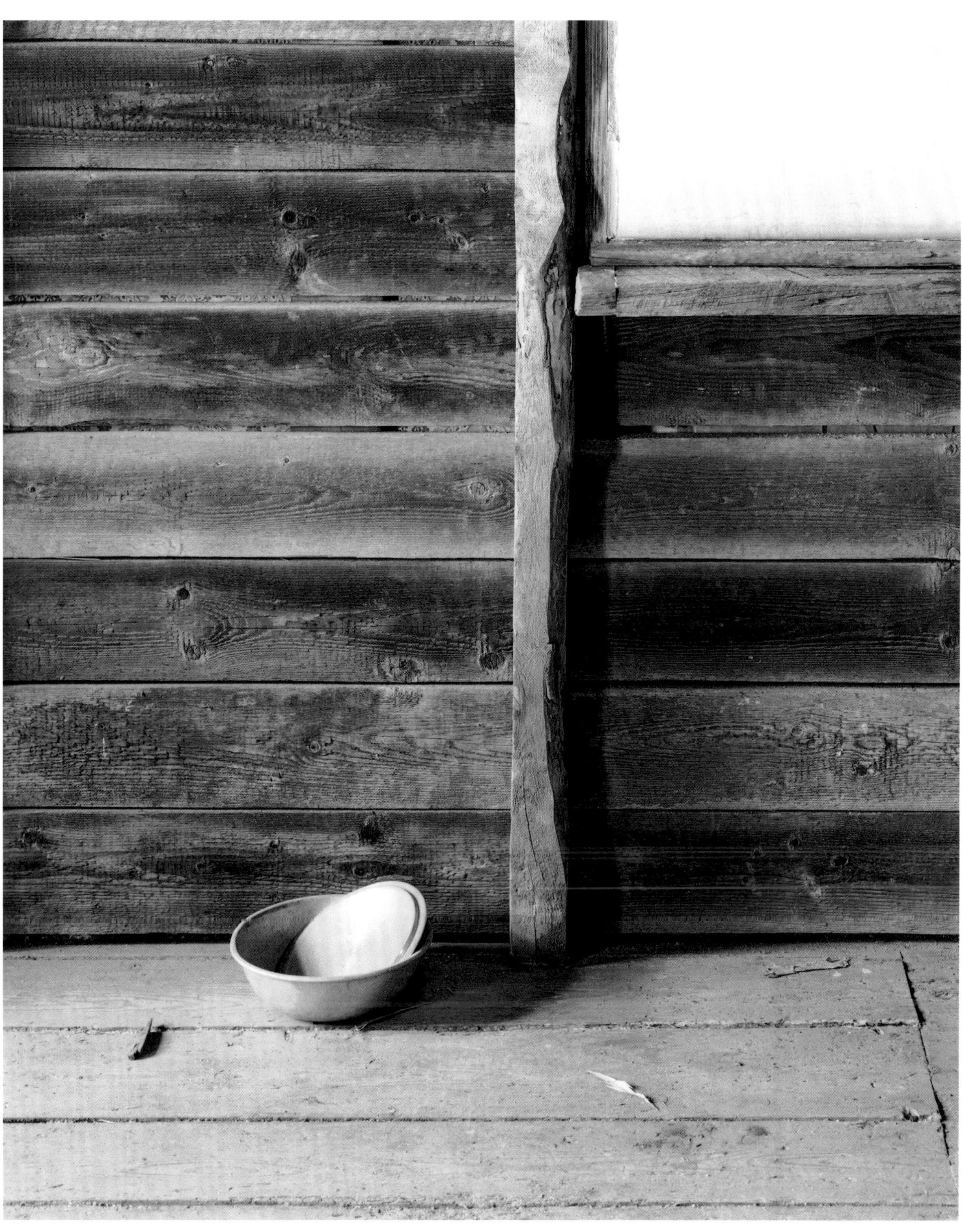

Metal Cups
2013

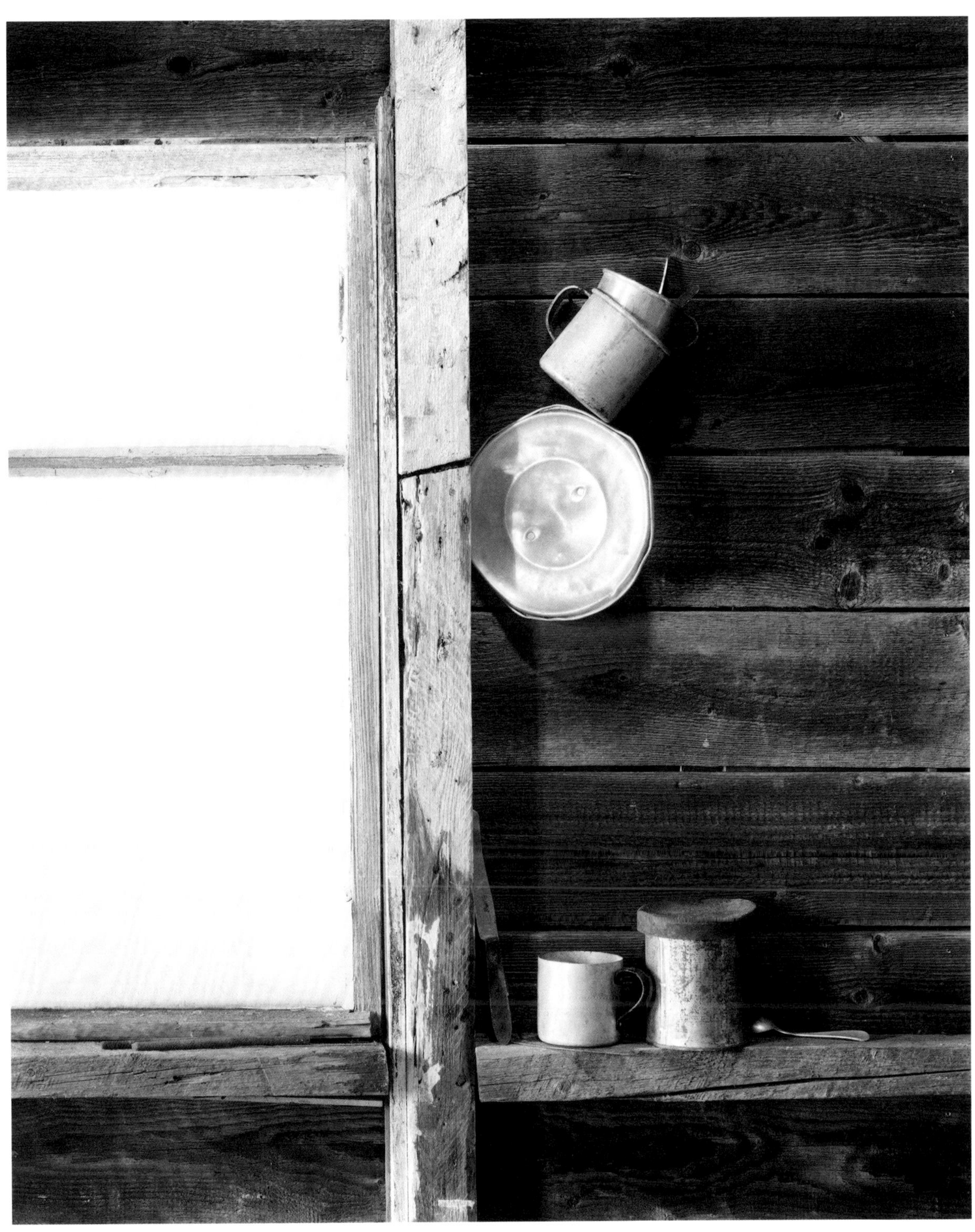

Towel
2013

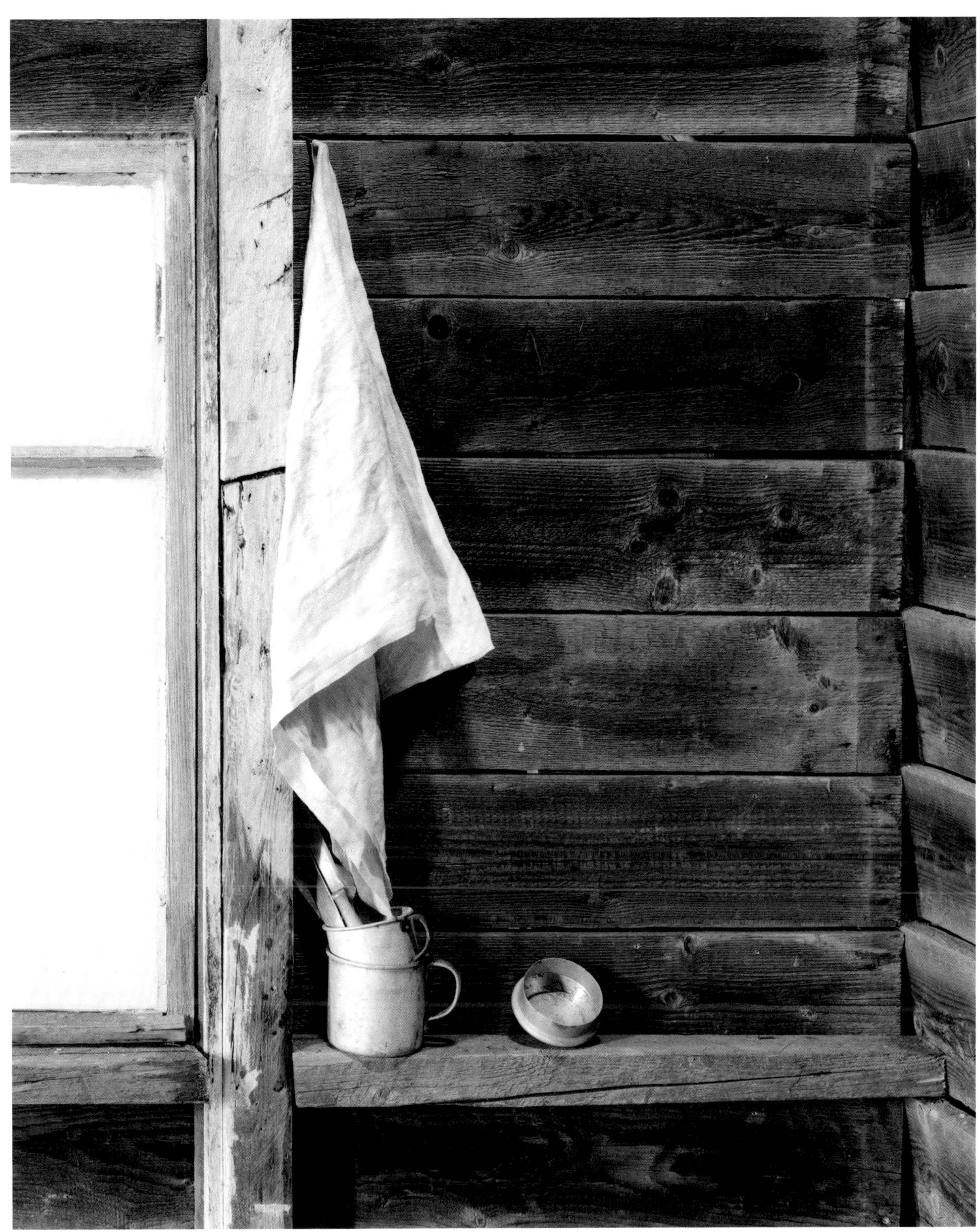

Bucket
2013

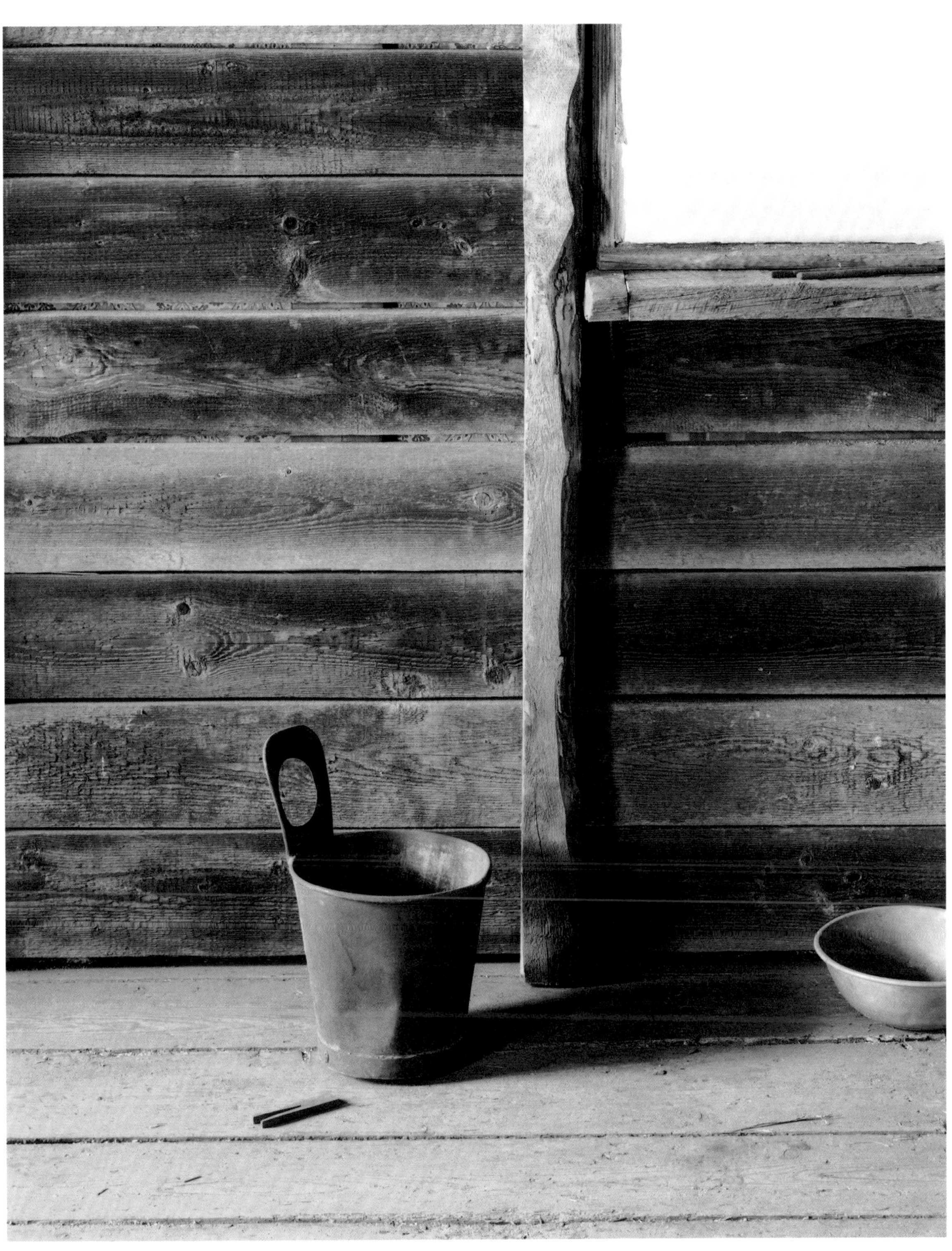

Picture (No. 2)
2013

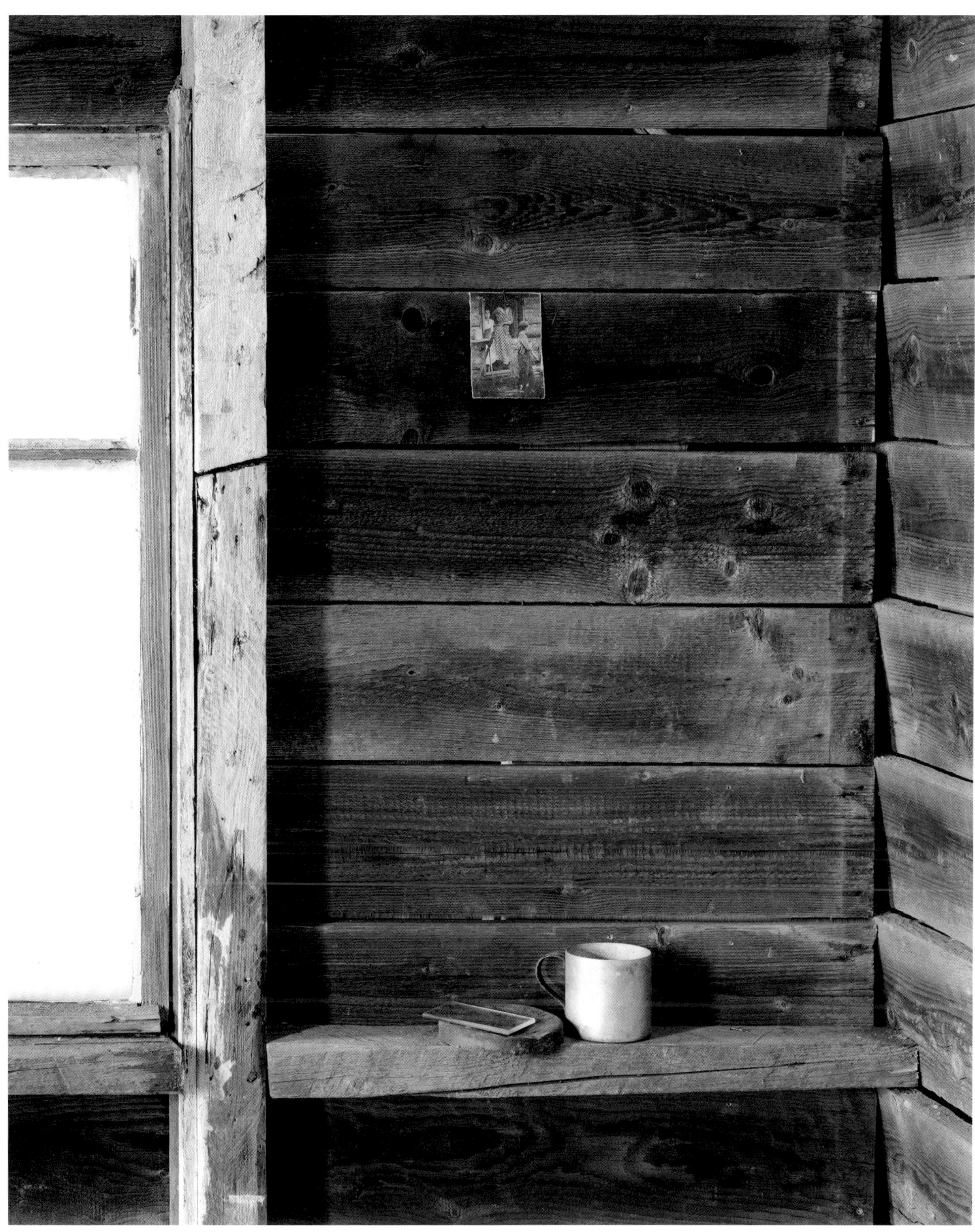

Clothes Peg
2013

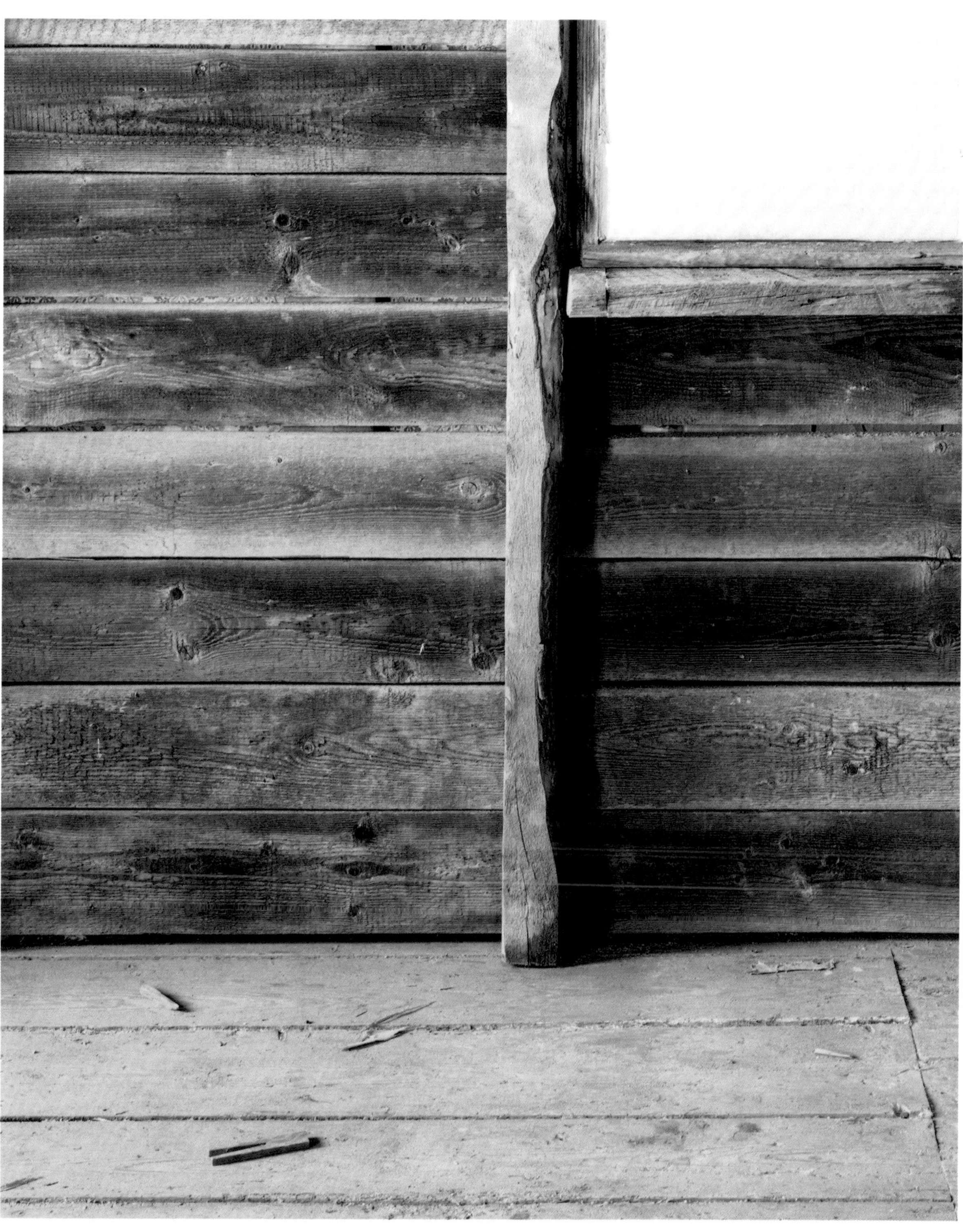

Pot
2013

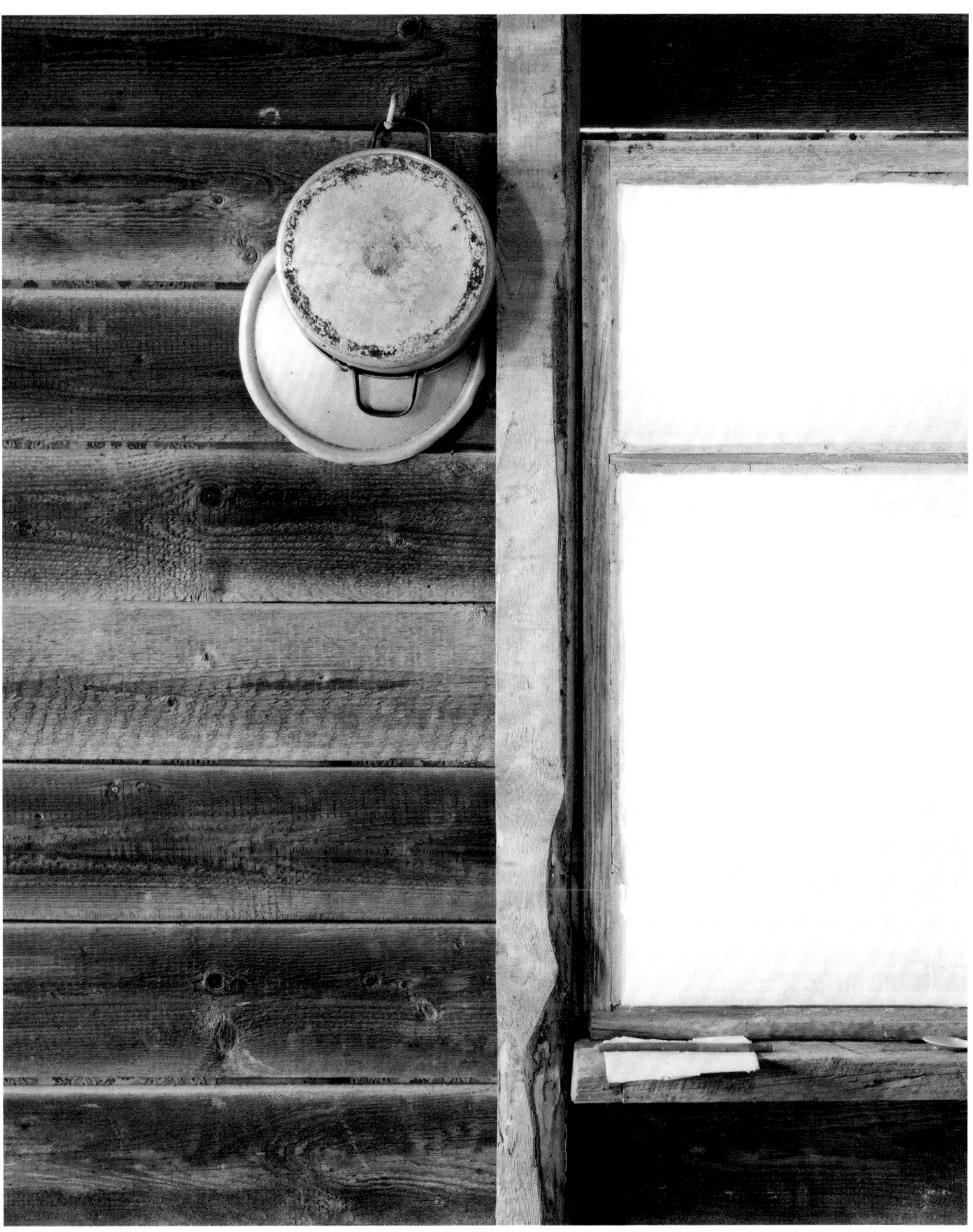

Werkliste / List of Works

7 *Ladder*
2011
Archival Inkjet Print
116 × 93 cm

9 *Cookware and Paper Bag*
2011
Archival Inkjet Print
116 × 93 cm

11 *Oil Can and Towel*
2011
Archival Inkjet Print
116 × 93 cm

13 *Dishes and Paper Bag*
2012
Archival Inkjet Print
116 × 93 cm

15 *Kitchen Wall*
2011
Gelatin Silver Print
57 × 47 cm

17 *Cookware and Towel*
2011
Archival Inkjet Print
116 × 93 cm

19 *Jerry Can and Bottle*
2011
Archival Inkjet Print
116 × 93 cm

21 *Bottle, Flatware and Pitcher*
2011
Gelatin Silver Print
58 × 47,5 cm

23 *Metal Cans*
2011
Gelatin Silver Print
58 × 47,5 cm

25 *Chair*
2011
Archival Inkjet Print
116 × 93 cm

27 *Bowl, Paper Bag and Pot*
2012
Archival Inkjet Print
116 × 93 cm

29 *Mirrors and Metal Cup*
2012
Gelatin Silver Print
57 × 47 cm

31 *Can and Rope*
2011
Archival Inkjet Print
116 × 93 cm

33 *Lid and Bowls*
2012
Gelatin Silver Print
58 × 47,5 cm

35 *Metal Can and Paper Bag*
2012
Gelatin Silver Print
58 × 47,5 cm

37 *Two Cans*
2011
Gelatin Silver Print
52 × 42 cm

39 *Dishes*
2012
Gelatin Silver Print
58 × 47,5 cm

41 *Paper Bag and Can*
2012
Gelatin Silver Print
58 × 47,5 cm

43 *Bottle and Lid*
2012
Gelatin Silver Print
48 × 59 cm

45 *Bottle*
2013
Archival Inkjet Print
62,5 × 51 cm

47 *Picture*
2013
Archival Inkjet Print
62,5 × 51 cm

49 *Tin*
2013
Archival Inkjet Print
62,5 × 51 cm

51 *Metal Cup*
2013
Archival Inkjet Print
62,5 × 51 cm

53 *Mirror*
2013
Archival Inkjet Print
62,5 × 51 cm

55 *Metal Bowl*
2013
Archival Inkjet Print
62,5 × 51 cm

57 *Metal Cups*
2013
Archival Inkjet Print
62,5 × 51 cm

59 *Towel*
2013
Archival Inkjet Print
62,5 × 51 cm

61 *Bucket*
2013
Archival Inkjet Print
62,5 × 51 cm

63 *Picture (No. 2)*
2013
Archival Inkjet Print
62,5 × 51 cm

65 *Clothes Peg*
2013
Archival Inkjet Print
62,5 × 51 cm

67 *Pot*
2013
Archival Inkjet Print
62,5 × 51 cm

Re-Inszenierungen: Vorbild, Nachbau, Nachbild

Matthias Harder

Oskar Schmidt analysiert, seziert und re-inszeniert gewisse Aspekte der Fotografiegeschichte, beispielsweise Aufnahmen von Walker Evans, die dieser im Auftrag der Farm Security Administration, kurz: FSA, in den 1930er Jahren im Süden der USA anfertigte. In *The American Series* greift Schmidt diese Ikonen der klassischen Fotoreportage des vergangenen Jahrhunderts auf, konkret Evans' Bildserie von Bud Fields Haus in Hale County, Alabama, aus dem Jahr 1936. Dieser Ort steht symbolisch für die Nachrezessionszeit in Amerika.

Oskar Schmidts kluge und spielerische Untersuchung von Realität und deren Abbild transformiert eine historische, sozialdokumentarische Bildidee in dessen heutiges Künstleratelier. Doch was sehen wir überhaupt auf den schlichten Schwarz-Weiß-Fotografien? Schauen wir uns exemplarisch eine Aufnahme genauer an: Auf einem Hochformat mit dem schlichten englischen Titel *Kitchen Wall* sehen wir als Hauptbildgegenstand ein unvollständiges Essbesteck, das hinter einem an eine Holzwand gehefteten Holzstück steckt. Es ist ein angelaufenes, schmutziges, teilweise verrostetes Besteck: vier Löffel und fünf Messer, eines davon ohne Griff. Gabeln existieren anscheinend nicht in diesem ärmlichen Haushalt, dafür hängt am Ende des flachen dunklen Riegels noch eine Blechtasse. Darin, ebenso wie in dem Metall zweier Teelöffel, reflektiert sich Licht, das von außen in die Holzhütte einzudringen scheint. Die Lichtquelle selbst, vermutlich ein Fenster oder eine Tür, sehen wir hingegen nicht; so bleibt es ein in sich geschlossener Raum oder vielmehr eine Raumecke. Zwei Holzlattenwände stoßen im rechten Winkel aufeinander, die Holzbalken der Innenwand sind weder gegen die Unbill des Wetters gedämmt noch mit Bildern geschmückt, sondern schlicht hell lasiert. Das Schwarz-Weiß der Aufnahme muss hier keine Transformation aus der Lokalfarbigkeit bedeuten. Denn wir könnten uns jene Hütte und das Besteck auch exakt in ebendieser Farbigkeit – oder Nicht-Farbigkeit der vielfältigen Grautöne – vorstellen. Von den Bewohnern gibt es keine (weitere) Spur. Normalerweise werden Besteck und Geschirr in Schränken aufbewahrt, doch sind solche Möbel wahrscheinlich in dieser Hütte nicht vorhanden. Ein wenig rechts oberhalb des Bestecks befindet sich ein horizontaler Querbalken, der die vertikalen Holzlatten zu stabilisieren, aber ansonsten keine weitere statische Funktion für das Gebäude zu haben scheint. Die Oberfläche der Holzlatten ist rau, und viele kleine schwarze Flecken beleben die Innenwände visuell. Die wenigen Dinge, die wir sehen, oder besser: die uns Schmidt zu sehen gibt, können in solchen menschenleeren Aufnahmen stellvertretend für den abwesenden Benutzer inklusive Abnutzungsspuren, also auch Zeitspuren, angesehen werden.

So wie das Bild – im überlegten Austarieren von Vertikalen und Horizontalen – genauestens komponiert ist, so arrangiert der Künstler seine Arbeiten an der Wand des Ausstellungsraumes mit großer Präzision. Die Fotografien ergänzen sich dort, ohne ihre Autonomie zu verlieren. Durch die Größe des Abzuges steuert Schmidt in unserer Wahrnehmung den Realitätsgehalt: Sind die Messer etwa genauso groß wie in Wirklichkeit, wird das Bild eher zu einer Art Fenster als zu einer bloßen Umsetzung des Vorhandenen. Das zeitlose Schwarz-Weiß verschiebt die Wirkung jedoch ins Historische.

Restagings: Model, Replica, Afterimage

Matthias Harder

Oskar Schmidt analyzes, dissects, and restages certain aspects of photo history, like the photographs of Walker Evans, for example, that were created for the U.S. Farm Security Administration (FSA) in the South of the USA in the 1930s. In his *The American Series* Schmidt takes on these icons of classic photojournalism of the past decades, specifically Evans's photo series of Bud Fields's house in Hale County, Alabama, from 1936. This place is emblematic of the post-Depression era in the United States.

Oskar Schmidt's astute and playful investigation of reality and its likeness transforms a historic, social-documentary concept in his present-day artist's studio. But what do we actually see in these stark black-and-white photographs? Let us examine one exemplary photograph more closely: in a portrait-format shot with the simple title *Kitchen Wall* we see an incomplete set of cutlery tucked behind a piece of wood attached to the timber wall as the main subject of the image. The flatware is tarnished, dirty, and partly rusted: four spoons and five knives, one of which has no handle. Forks appear not to exist in this poverty-stricken household, there is however a tin cup hanging at the end of the flat dark strip. Here, like in the pair of metal teaspoons, light is reflected, which seems to permeate into the wooden cabin from outside. But the light source itself, probably a window or a door, is not seen; thus it remains a self-contained space, or in fact a corner of a room. Two wooden-slat walls meet each other in the right-hand corner, the timber beams of the interior wall are neither insulated against the harshness of the weather nor decorated with pictures, its finish simple and bright. The black and white of the photograph does not necessarily mean a transformation from the local color. As we could also imagine the cabin and the flatware with exactly this same coloring—or rather the non-coloring of these varying shades of gray. Of the inhabitants there is no (other) trace. Usually cutlery and dishes are stored in cabinets, but such furnishings are probably not to be found in this cabin. A little to the right above the flatware there is a horizontal crossbeam that stabilizes the vertical wooden slats, but otherwise seems to have no other structural function in the building. The surface of the wooden slats is raw; flecks of black visually activate the interior walls. In a photograph empty of people such as this, the few things that we see, or that Schmidt allows us to see, can be considered as standing in for the absent inhabitant and their traces of wear, thus also the traces of time.

Just like this image is precisely composed, in the deliberate balance of verticals and horizontals, the artist arranges his works on the wall of the exhibition space with great precision. The photographs complement each other, without losing their autonomy. Through the size of the prints Schmidt controls the contents of reality in our perception: the knives are roughly the same size as in reality, the photo becoming more a kind of window than a mere permutation of what already exists. However, the timeless black and white shifts the effect into the historic.

The American Appropriation artist Sherrie Levine had already made works "after Evans" and his FSA photographs in 1981 and also remained in the black-and-white spectrum with her appropriated, reproduced images of the wooden cabins. Admittedly, she did not restage the settings, instead within her technically heterogeneous works she fundamentally challenged the creation of original art with these directly appropriated images; indeed, she sometimes denied the rele-

Die amerikanische Appropriationkünstlerin Sherrie Levine hat bereits 1981 „nach Evans" und dessen FSA-Aufnahmen gearbeitet und blieb mit den angeeigneten, reproduzierten Bildern der Holzhütten ebenfalls im Schwarz-Weiß-Spektrum. Allerdings re-inszenierte sie nicht die Situation, sondern stellte mit solchen unmittelbaren Bildübernahmen innerhalb ihres medial heterogenen Werks das Erschaffen von originärer Kunst grundsätzlich infrage, ja, sie leugnete mitunter die Relevanz der Urheberschaft eines Kunstwerks. Oskar Schmidt hingegen eignet sich zwar ebenfalls eine Bildidee an, formuliert und deutet sie jedoch um – und erweitert damit unsere Rezeption. Im Gegensatz zu Levine begegnet der Betrachter einer Neuschöpfung.

Die Authentizität ist aber auch hier, in dieser grundsätzlichen Untersuchung von Bildern durch Bilder, nur simuliert. Was genau passiert in der Wiederholung, durch eine motivische Übernahme oder Annäherung? Bei Schmidt wirkt im direkten Bildvergleich zu Evans und Levine alles ein bisschen aufgeräumter und perfekter. In einer solchen Perfektion zeigt sich die Paraphrasierung des Realen in der Nachschöpfung.

Der in Berlin und Leipzig lebende Künstler baut Kulissen für seine Fotografien. Man könnte behaupten: Er hält sich nicht mehr auf mit der Realität. Andere Kommilitonen der Leipziger Hochschule für Grafik und Buchkunst aus der inzwischen legendären Klasse von Timm Rautert arbeiten ähnlich: Falk Haberkorn etwa räumte in stundenlanger Arbeit erst ein kleines Waldstück auf, bevor er es analog fotografierte. Natürlich ließe sich das gleiche Bildergebnis ebenfalls mit Hilfe von Photoshop erreichen, doch er legt selbst Hand an – und beschwört enigmatisch mit seinen großformatigen Schwarz-Weiß-Aufnahmen Reste des Authentischen. Ähnlich geht Ricarda Roggan vor: Für eine Werkgruppe bedeckte sie sorgfältig mehrere Unfallautos so gleichmäßig mit Staub, dass bei uns der Eindruck entsteht, als stünden diese schon lange in der titelgebenden „Garage" und würden nur auf eine Reparatur warten. Die Art der fotografischen Inszenierung gerät bei Roggan, Haberkorn und Schmidt zur Bühnensituation. Es kommt allerdings zu einer gewissen Verschiebung im Verhältnis zwischen der Darstellung von Alltagsgegenständen und deren leicht Irritation auslösende Rezeption.

So unterschiedlich die Themen sind, so unterschiedlich verläuft das Aneignen, Nachstellen, Kopieren oder paraphrasierende Zitieren früherer Fotografie. Oskar Schmidt orientiert sich an einem von ihm gewählten ikonischen Vorbild, baut es aufwendig in Lebensgröße nach und bildet es ab, indem er sich auf Details und deren Materialoberflächen konzentriert. Der dreidimensionale Nachbau eines Raumes 1:1, also das interpretierende Nach-Bild als Vorbild für die Fotografie, ist als eigenständiges Werk für den Künstler irrelevant. Das bringt Schmidts Arbeitsweise der *The American Series* in die Nähe derer von Thomas Demand. Ein Raum entsteht bei beiden zu dem einzigen Zweck, ihn anschließend zu fotografieren; beide erschaffen – und spielen mit – Illusion. Die so entstehende Kulisse entspricht einer verschobenen Wirklichkeit, ist die bloße Konstruktion einer Wahrheit. Oskar Schmidt verzichtet zudem bewusst darauf, Fehler mithilfe digitaler Postproduktion einzubauen. Allerdings interpretiert er die gewählte visuelle Vorlage in Bezug auf den Aufbau und die Komposition des Bildes – und verändert sie. Der Anspruch auf Authentizität innerhalb des Mediums Fotografie hat sich schon seit langem auf einen kümmerlichen Rest reduziert. Nichtsdestotrotz sind manche Fotografen heute, jenseits realitätsgetreuer Abbildungsideale, auf der Suche nach dem (nahezu) perfekten Bild. Immer ist bei Schmidts *The American Series* die Idee der hohen Stilisierung von Gegenstand und Raum, in sorgsam austarierten

vance of the authorship of a work of art. Oskar Schmidt likewise appropriates the pictorial concept, but reformulates and reinterprets it—and thus expands our reception. In contrast to Levine, the viewer encounters a new creation.

But here, in this strict examination of photos through photos, the authenticity is also just simulated. What happens exactly in the repetition, through thematic appropriation or approximation? In direct comparison to the images by Evans and Levine, everything in Schmidt's photographs appears a bit cleaned up and more perfect. In such perfection the paraphrasing of the real is reflected in the re-creation.

The artist, who lives in Berlin and Leipzig, builds backdrops for his photographs. One could contend that he is no longer constrained with reality. His fellow students from Timm Rautert's now legendary class at the Leipzig Academy of Visual Arts work in a similar manner: Falk Haberkorn, for example, clears a small section of forest over several hours before he photographs it via analog means. Of course, the same result can also be reached with help from Photoshop, nevertheless he himself takes up the task—and enigmatically evokes the remnants of the authentic with his large-format black-and-white photographs. Ricarda Roggan takes a similar approach in *Garage:* for this series of works she carefully coats several wrecked cars with an even layer of dust, so that they appear to have stood for a long time in the garage of the title, waiting to be repaired. The kind of photographic staging by Roggan, Haberkorn, and Schmidt becomes a mise en scène. This results though in a certain shifting of the relationship between the representation of everyday objects, and their slightly irritation-provoking reception.

As the themes are different, the appropriation, reconstruction, copying, or paraphrasing of early photography proceeds differently too. Based on an iconic original of his choosing, Oskar Schmidt re-creates it elaborately in life-size, reproducing it with a focus on its details and material surfaces. The 1:1 three-dimensional replica of a room, thus the interpretive "after image" as a model for photography, is irrelevant as a stand-alone work for the artist. This brings Schmidt's approach in his *The American Series* close to that of Thomas Demand. For both a space is created for the same purpose, to subsequently be photographed; both create—and play with—illusion. The resulting backdrop corresponds to a suspended reality—the mere construction of a truth. Oskar Schmidt consciously foregoes building in mistakes by means of digital post-production. However, he interprets the chosen visual template in regards to the construction and composition of the image—and alters it. The claim of authenticity within the medium of photography has already been reduced to a meager remnant for some time. Nonetheless many photographers today, beyond true-to-reality ideals of reproduction, seek the (nearly) perfect image. In Schmidt's *The American Series* the concept of high stylization of objects and space in carefully balanced relationships to one another is always evident. The artist lends an identity to every space with the simplest of means.

Only on second look, or respectively with the knowledge of the model-like quality of the photo set, do we understand: here nothing is as it seems. It is not a reproduction of reality; everything is a backdrop, which is in turn, like the light, absolutely real. And so there is a blurring of aspects of the representation of reality, of the staging or restaging. The deliberate derivation is, as a matter of course, not based on plagiarism; it is a paraphrased visual quotation. Oskar Schmidt confuses our perception, and with these methods he plunges us into doubt. This is not predicated on a freezing of time genuine to photography, but rather on one of

Beziehungen zueinander, spürbar. Jedem Raum verleiht der Künstler mit geringsten Mitteln eine Identität.

Erst auf den zweiten Blick respektive mit dem Wissen um die Modellhaftigkeit der Aufnahmesituation verstehen wir: Hier ist nichts, wie es scheint. Es ist keine Abbildung der Realität, alles ist Kulisse, die allerdings wiederum wie auch das Licht durchaus real ist. So verschwimmen die Aspekte der Wirklichkeitsdarstellung, der Inszenierung oder Re-Inszenierung. Der bewussten Nachschöpfung liegt selbstverständlich kein Plagiat zugrunde, sondern ein paraphrasierendes Bildzitat. Oskar Schmidt verwirrt unsere Wahrnehmung, er stürzt uns mit dieser Methode in Zweifel. Dahinter steht nicht das der Fotografie genuine Einfrieren von Zeit, eher das einer augenblicksunabhängigen Zeitlichkeit. Der Dualismus von Realität und Künstlichkeit wird aufgehoben. Es ist stets beides zugleich.

Der Verzicht auf inhaltliche Brüche oder ein zusätzliches Dekor unterstreicht das Authentische oder besser: Schmidts Spiel mit dem Authentischen. Es herrscht eine geradezu klinische Schärfe in seinen Aufnahmen der Bildräume, die in die Fläche komprimiert erscheinen. So verschwinden keine Bilddetails in einer möglichen Unschärfe, vielmehr positioniert Schmidt die Gegenstände häufig nach den jahrhundertealten Regeln des sogenannten Goldenen Schnitts. Was wie eine beiläufige Aufnahme eines Schuppens oder der Wand einer kargen Holzhütte erscheint, ist tatsächlich bis ins Letzte durchdacht. Alle Bildelemente sind exakt austariert, auf Blickwinkel und Oberflächenbeschaffenheit hin überprüft. Auch die Graustufen in den Bildern sind variantenreich durchdekliniert.

In weiteren Aufnahmen dieser groß angelegten und über einen Zeitraum von mehreren Jahren verfolgten *The American Series* sehen wir auch andere Räume der amerikanischen Holzhütte, die in Schmidts Atelier aus groben Holzlatten nachgebaut wurden.

Die vermeintliche Veranda in *Ladder,* ebenfalls 2011 realisiert und grundsätzlich einer Walker-Evans-Aufnahme nicht unähnlich, markiert die nur schwer zu definierende Zone zwischen Innen und Außen. Auch in diesem ruhigen Bild besticht die klare Gliederung mit den wenigen arrangierten Alltagsgegenständen, die unsere Aufmerksamkeit erregen: der titelgebenden, selbstgezimmerten Holzleiter, einem kleinen leeren Blecheimer links daneben und einem Metallkanister dahinter. Die Verdichtung von drei so zeitlosen Gegenständen im Bildraum wird durch dessen grundsätzliche Leere konterkariert. Wieder ist kein Mensch zu sehen, kein Bewohner oder Gast des Hauses. Für die Leiter scheint das gleiche Holz verwendet worden zu sein wie für den Boden der Veranda oder die Wände der Hütte; so scheint sie teilweise mit der Wand zu verschmelzen. Das Licht dringt von links ins Bild und lässt die Dinge diffuse Schatten werfen und einen immateriellen Bildraum erschaffen. Es ist kein öffentlicher, sondern ein privater Raum – wie immer nur ein kleiner Ausschnitt aus einem Umraum, den wir nicht sehen, aber unmittelbar imaginieren können, auch wenn die Imagination uns in die Irre führt. Der Blick ins Innere der Hütte durch die geöffnete Tür bleibt schwarz, beim genauen Hinsehen entdecken wir in der dunklen Fläche eine geringe Zeichnung, als befände sich dort ein Raum oder eine zweite Ebene. Tatsächlich ist dort nichts, Nicht-Raum, Nicht-Besitz, keine Zeit oder Erinnerung, eine negative Utopie. Die Modellhaftigkeit der Schmidt'schen Inszenierung wird zum Prinzip radikaler Reduktion.

Die harten Lebensbedingungen der Familie Field in Alabama, damals festgehalten von Walker Evans, werden hier in eine menschenleere, fast künstliche Scheinwelt übersetzt. Oskar Schmidt entpersonalisiert in seinem Bildzitat das Beziehungsgeflecht aus Armutsdarstellung und deren Rezeption. Medial interessant

a temporality independent of the present moment. The dualism of reality and artificiality is voided. It is always both simultaneously.

The eschewal of breaks in content or additional decoration underscores the authentic, or indeed, Schmidt's play with the authentic. An almost clinical sharpness prevails in his photographs of pictorial spaces, which appear compressed across the surface. Thus no details disappear into a possible uncertainty, rather Schmidt often positions the objects according to the centuries-old rules of the so-called Golden Ratio. What seems like a casual photograph of a shanty or the wall of a barren wooden cabin, is actually thoroughly considered down to the last detail. All elements of the image are exactly balanced, every angle and surface characteristic scrutinized. Also the various shades of gray are fully inflected in the images.

In further photographs of the large-scale and long-term *The American Series* we see other spaces of the American cabin re-created in Schmidt's studio from rough wooden slats.

The ostensible veranda in *Ladder,* also realized in 2011 and essentially not dissimilar to a Walker Evans photograph, marks the hard-to-define zone between inside and outside. The clear structure stands out in this quiet image with sparsely arranged everyday objects which attract our attention: the titular hand-built wooden ladder, a small empty metal bucket to its left, and behind it a metal canister. The consolidation of three such timeless objects in the composition is counteracted through their fundamental emptiness. Again, no person is seen, no resident or guest appears in the house. The same wood seems to have been used for the ladder as for the flooring of the veranda and the walls of the cabin; thus it seems to partly blend into the wall. The light penetrates from the left into the image letting the objects cast diffuse shadows and creating an immaterial pictorial space. It is not public, but rather a private space—as always it is only a small cutout from the surrounding space that we do not see, but can immediately imagine, even if the imagination leads us astray. The view into the interior of the cabin through the opened door remains black; on closer look we discover in this dark area a slight outline, as if there were a room or a second level. Actually there is nothing, a non-room, non-domain, no time or memory, a negative utopia. The model-like quality of Schmidt's staging is the principle of radical reduction.

The hard conditions of life for the Fields family in Alabama, captured at the time by Walker Evans, are translated here into an uninhabited, almost artificial illusory world. In his pictorial quotation Oskar Schmidt depersonalizes the interplay between the representation of poverty and its reception. Interesting in respect to the medium is the contemporary long-distance appropriation of such motifs, virtually, as it were. While earlier photographers still traveled half the world to investigate and photograph on site, the approach to subject matter has since become virtualized. Oskar Schmidt does not even have to leave the studio in order to appropriate the world (and the history of photography)—as done here with the Southern United States.

The investigation of the subject goes also beyond an exposed stylization to an examination of the media. Through Oskar Schmidt's keen eye for the composition there is only an image from the constructed illusory space. And that which is transitory, that which is inherent to the world and its phenomena and can be so superbly visualized by the medium of photography, becomes especially apparent in such juxtapositions of historic and contemporary images.

ist die heutige Aneignung solcher Bildmotive über große Entfernungen, gleichsam virtuell. Während Fotografen früher noch um den halben Erdball reisten, um vor Ort zu recherchieren und zu fotografieren, hat sich die Annäherung an einen Bildgegenstand inzwischen virtualisiert. Oskar Schmidt verlässt nicht einmal mehr das Studio, um sich die Welt (und die Fotografiegeschichte) anzueignen – hier den Süden der USA.

Die Untersuchung des Gegenstandes wird jenseits einer exponierten Stilisierung auch zur Überprüfung des Medialen. Durch Oskar Schmidts genauen Blick für die Komposition wird aus dem gebauten Illusionsraum erst ein Bild. Und das Transitorische, das der Welt und ihren Erscheinungen innewohnt und vom Medium Fotografie so hervorragend visuell umgesetzt werden kann, wird in solchen Gegenüberstellungen von historischen und zeitgenössischen Bildern besonders sichtbar.

Die Dramaturgie der Objekte *The American Series* von Oskar Schmidt

Renate Wiehager

Jedes Wort, jedes Bild ist gepachtet und belehnt.
Wir wissen, dass ein Bild nur ein Raum ist,
in dem die verschiedensten Bilder – keines von ihnen ein Original –
aufeinanderprallen und verschmelzen.
Ein Bild ist ein Gewebe von Zitaten aus den zahllosen Zentren der Kultur.
(Sherrie Levine, 1982)[1]

Walker Evans, *Fireplace in Floyd Burroughs's Bedroom with Bedpost in Foreground, Hale County, Alabama,* 1936

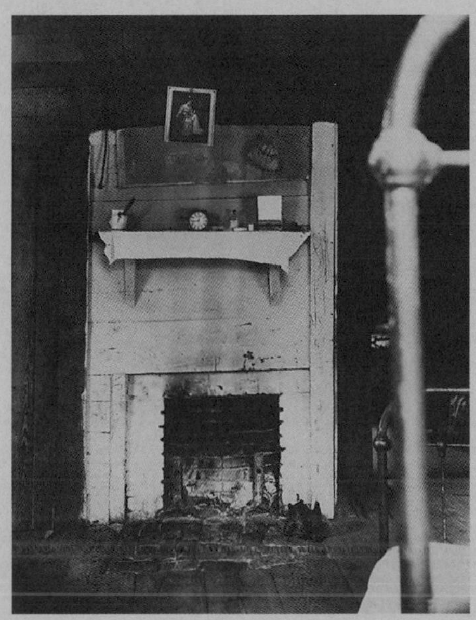

Sherrie Levine, *After Walker Evans: 9,* 1981

Der nachfolgende Text unternimmt den Versuch, die zwischen 2011 und 2013 entstandene, rund 40 Motive umfassende Arbeit *The American Series* von Oskar Schmidt in ihren sowohl kunst- wie fotohistorisch komplexen Bezügen vorzustellen. Neben den fotografischen Vorlagen von Walker Evans aus den 1930er Jahren wird erstmals auch die Bedeutung der konzeptuellen Fotoarbeiten von Sherrie Levine näher ins Auge gefasst.

Die Titel kunstkritischer Essays zu den frühen Ausstellungen Sherrie Levines um 1980 – „Pictures and Meaning", „The Allegorical Impulse", „Too Good to Be True", „It's Not Fake Anything – It's Real Levine" – reflektieren die kontrovers geführte Debatte um Original versus Kopie, Unikat versus Wiederholung. Neben Objekten und Bildern, die kunsthistorische Vorbilder des 20. Jahrhunderts kopierten, war Levine vor allem mit aus Büchern abfotografierten Werken berühmter Fotografen wie Edward Weston und Walker Evans hervorgetreten. In ihrem wegweisenden Essay „Die Originalität der Avantgarde" (1981)[2] wählte Rosalind Krauss das Werk von Levine als zentrales, da radikalstes Beispiel von „Raubfotografie", „Diskurs der Kopie" und postmodernistischer Strategie.

Die enorme kunsttheoretische Bedeutung der *After Walker Evans*-Serie von Sherrie Levine verbindet sich mit dem Kontext ihrer ersten öffentlichen Präsentationen und der Radikalität ihrer Geste. Die 1979 eröffnete Galerie Metro Pictures in New York, wo Levines Fotoserie 1981 zuerst ausgestellt wurde, sammelte um sich Künstler, die als Begründer der Appropriation Art galten (Troy Brauntuch, Robert Longo, Richard Prince, Cindy Sherman u.a.) und als „The Pictures Generation" wesentlich die Kunstdiskussion der frühen 1980er Jahre geprägt haben.[3] Als radikal wurde selbst in diesem künstlerischen Umfeld, welches die Ubiquität der Bilder und die Entwertung von Original und Autorschaft vor Augen führte, Sherrie Levines analytische Strategie empfunden: das Abfotografieren ikonischer Bilder der Fotohistorie des frühen 20. Jahrhunderts und deren motivisch unveränderte Präsentation. Wobei, eine konzeptuell signifikante Entscheidung, Levine für ihre Fotografien die Größe der Katalogabbildungen wählt, statt das Format der Originale von Evans zu zitieren: Die Künstlerin demonstriert damit, dass ihre Fotografien Kopien von Reproduktionen (aus Büchern) sind, welche „Originale" abbilden, die ihrerseits auf motivischen Anleihen von Gemälden eines sozialkritischen Realismus des 19. Jahrhunderts basieren (man denke an die Darstellungen bäuerlicher Armut in den Bildern eines Gustave Courbet, Adolf Menzel oder Jean-François Millet). Die Kopie der Kopie der Kopie unterminiert und stimuliert das Bilddenken der Gegenwart.

The Dramaturgy of Objects
The American Series by Oskar Schmidt

Renate Wiehager

Every word, every image, is leased and mortgaged.
We know that a picture is but a
space in which a variety of images, none of them original,
blend and clash. A picture is a tissue of quotations
drawn from the innumerable centers of culture.
(Sherrie Levine, 1982)[1]

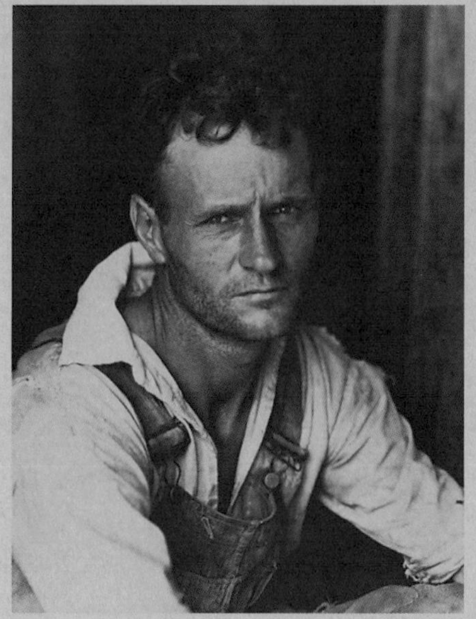

Sherrie Levine, *After Walker Evans: 3*, 1981

The following text endeavors to present the complex art- and photo-historic implications of *The American Series* by Oskar Schmidt, a work consisting of around 40 motifs created between 2011 and 2013. In addition to the photographic originals of Walker Evans from the 1930s, the significance of the conceptual photo works of Sherrie Levine for Schmidt's series will also be closely considered for the first time. The titles of art critical essays on the early exhibitions of Sherrie Levine from around 1980—"Pictures and Meaning," "The Allegorical Impulse," "Too Good to Be True," "It's Not Fake Anything—It's Real Levine,"—reflect the controversial debate on the original versus copy, unique object versus iteration. In addition to objects and images that copied art historical models of the 20th century, Levine became especially well known for re-photographing the works of famous photographers like Edward Weston and Walker Evans from books. In her groundbreaking essay "The Originality of the Avant-Garde" (1981)[2] Rosalind Krauss chose the work of Levine as the central, most radical example of "pirated photography," "discourse of the copy," and postmodernist strategy.

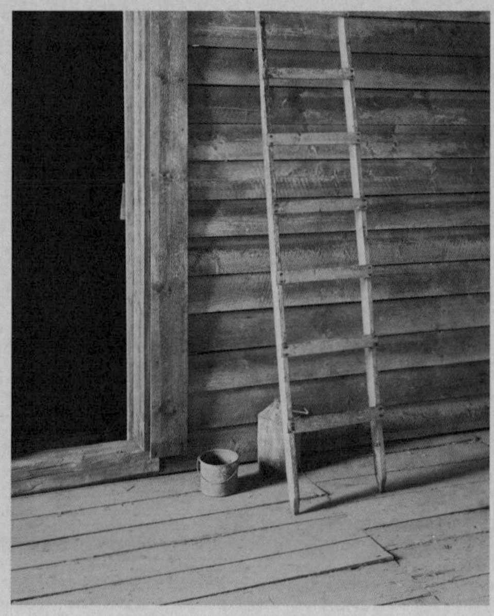

Oskar Schmidt, *Ladder*, 2011

The tremendous art historic significance of the *After Walker Evans* series by Sherrie Levine is intertwined with the context of her first public presentation and the radicalism of her gesture. Metro Pictures Gallery in New York, which opened in 1979 and was where Levine's photo series was first exhibited in 1981, brought together artists considered the founders of Appropriation art (Troy Brauntuch, Robert Longo, Richard Prince, Cindy Sherman, among others) and as "The Pictures Generation" fundamentally shaped the art discussion of the early 1980s.[3] In this artistic milieu, which demonstrated the ubiquity of the image and the devaluing of the original and authorship, even Sherrie Levine's analytical strategy was found to be radical: the photographing of iconic images from early 20th century photo history and their presentation as unchanged motifs. Levine, in a conceptually significant decision, sized her photographs to the catalog illustrations, instead of invoking the format of the original by Evans: the artist thus demonstrates that her photographs are copies of reproductions (in books) that depict "originals," which for their part are based on motifs borrowed from social-critical realist paintings of the 19th century (think of the representation of peasant penury in the paintings of Gustave Courbet, Adolf Menzel, or Jean-François Millet). The copy of the copy of the copy undermines and stimulates contemporary pictorial thinking.

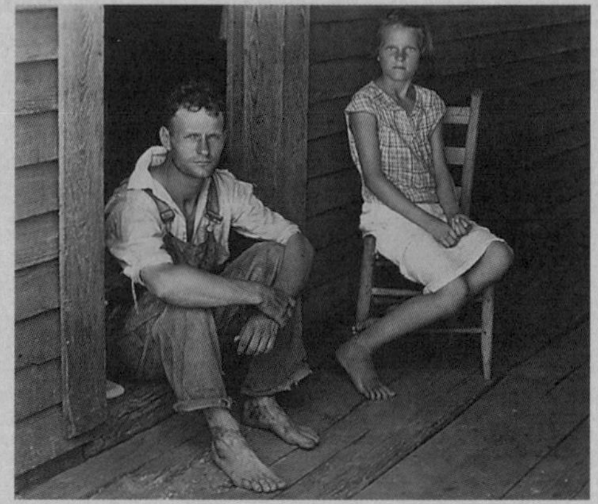

Walker Evans, *Floyd and Lucille Burroughs on Porch, Hale County, Alabama*, 1936

A look at the history of 20th-century photography quickly identifies the models that inspired Oskar Schmidt's series of staged black-and-white photographs entitled *The American Series:* Walker Evans's photographic social studies of America's

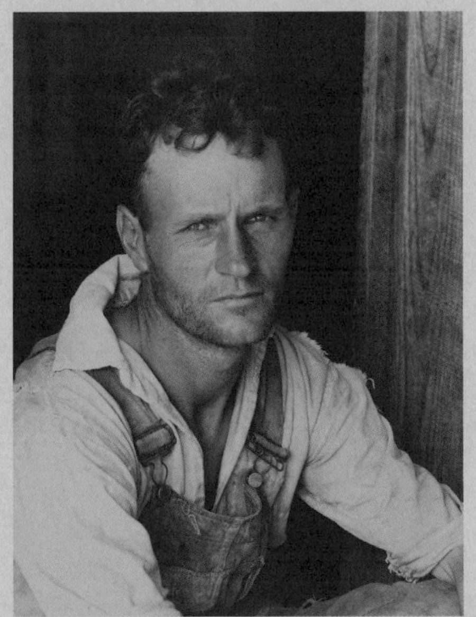

Walker Evans, *Alabama Tenant Farmer*, 1936

Die Geschichte der Fotografie des 20. Jahrhunderts vor Augen, vermag man schnell die Ausgangspunkte für Oskar Schmidts inszenierte Schwarz-Weiß-Fotografien aus *The American Series* auszumachen: Walker Evans fotografische Sozialstudien der amerikanischen Great Depression, 1936, wie auch Sherrie Levines konzeptuelle Aneignungen des Jahres 1981. Bevor aber diese Bezüge erläutert werden, soll zuerst der Weg einer genaueren Betrachtung der Fotografien von Oskar Schmidt, ihrer Technik und „Präsentationsformate", genommen und über die für sie charakteristische „Dramaturgie der Objekte" gesprochen werden. Dem folgt eine Rückbindung an vorhergehende Serien, um mit einen knappen Exkurs zum dinghaften Existenzialismus in den Filmen Samuel Becketts zu schließen.

Formate, Auflagen, Technik

Oskar Schmidts analog aufgenommene Schwarz-Weiß-Fotografien kultivieren eine „altmeisterliche" Technik, nicht um der reinen technischen Könnerschaft willen, sondern weil der Künstler damit die atmosphärische und inhaltliche Dimension seiner Motive pointieren, intensivieren kann. Rund 40 Motive – entstanden zwischen 2011 und 2013 – umfasst die fotografische Arbeit *The American Series*. Eine Auswahl von sieben Motiven wurde 2011 veröffentlicht, als Edition *The American Series I–XII*. Jedes Motiv existiert in zwei unterschiedlichen Formaten. Zum einen im kleineren Blattformat der Editionsmappe, welche das Format der klassischen Fotoeditionsbox aufgreift, zum anderen in zwei verschiedenen Größen als Ausstellungsprints: Das große Format ist den Bildausschnitten der Veranda mit schwarzer Türöffnung vorbehalten, während für die Innenräume mit weißem Fenster und den nahsichtig gegebenen Objekten ein kleineres Format gewählt wurde. Die großen Formate sind als Archival Pigment Print auf dem matt glänzenden, speziell für Schwarz-Weiß-Aufnahmen perfektionierten Museo Silver Rag-Papier gedruckt. Die Dichte des Prints und der reiche Tonwertumfang vermitteln der Dunkelheit der Türöffnung eine nachgerade körperliche Tiefe und Substanz, während die Graustufen der Schatten, der Holzmaserungen und der angelaufenen, zerkratzten Oberflächen des Aluminiumgeschirrs von dunklem Grau bis in eine silberne Tonigkeit hinüberspielen. Für die kleineren Ausstellungsprints hat Oskar Schmidt die Technik des im Labor selbstgefertigten Silbergelatine-Abzugs gewählt (also in der Dunkelkammer entstanden und nicht, wie die größeren Formate, als digitaler Inkjetprint). Auch dies ein klassisches Verfahren, das Schwarz-Weiß-Fotografien eine leichte Sepiatönung gibt, ohne doch die Vielfalt der grau-silbern-metallischen Nuancen zu reduzieren.

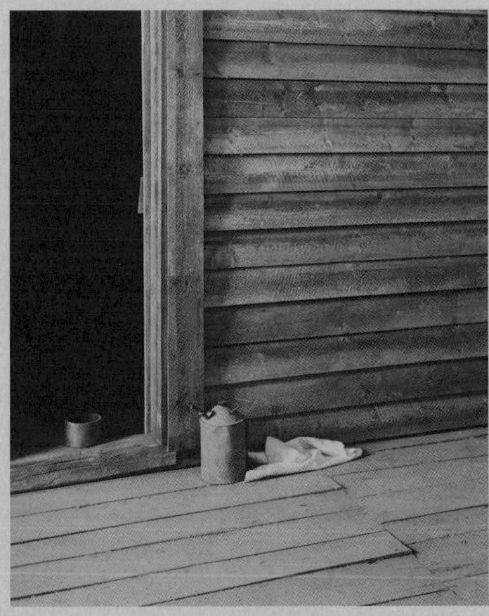

Oskar Schmidt, *Oil Can and Towel*, 2011

Nach den historischen Schwarz-Weiß-Aufnahmen der Familie Burroughs von Walker Evans – Teil einer ab 1936 im Auftrag entstandenen Serie über die sozialen Auswirkungen der wirtschaftlichen Depression in den amerikanischen Südstaaten – hat Oskar Schmidt im Atelier die Holzhütte der Familie Burroughs in Lebensgröße rekonstruiert. Mit einer analogen Großbildkamera gibt sich der Künstler selbst ein minimalistisches Setting: Variationen von Objekten vor und in der schwarzen Türöffnung auf der Veranda; Nahaufnahmen von Objekten; Interieurszenen um ein weiß überstrahltes Fenster herum.

Die Dramaturgie der Objekte

Das Moment einer ersten Faszination beim Betrachten der Bilder von Oskar Schmidt liegt in der scheinbaren Wiederholung des immer Gleichen bei höchster Ausdifferenzierung einer nicht-narrativen Detaillierung: Licht und Dunkelheit, farbig erscheinende Schatten und Tönungen, Texturen und Oberflächen, Leere

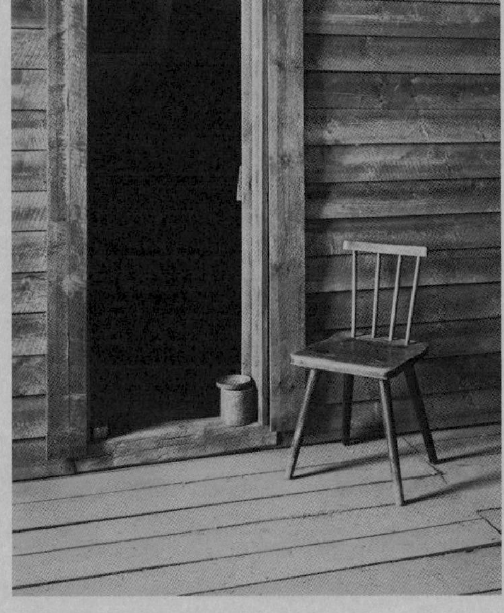

Oskar Schmidt, *Chair*, 2011

Great Depression era from 1936 and Sherrie Levine's conceptual appropriations from 1981. Before discussing these connections, however, I will take a closer look at Oskar Schmidt's photographs—at their technique, their "presentation formats" and at their characteristic "dramaturgy of objects." They will then be placed in relation to Schmidt's previous series. In conclusion, I will venture a brief digression on material existentialism in the films of Samuel Beckett.

Formats, Editions, Technique

Oskar Schmidt cultivates "Old Master" photographic techniques, not purely for the sake of technical skill, but because they allow him to distill and to intensify the atmospheric and thematic dimensions of his motifs. The photographic series *The American Series*—created between 2011 and 2013—comprises about 40 motifs. In 2011, a selection of seven motifs was published as *The American Series I–XII.* Each of these motifs exists in two different formats: first, in a small format in an edition portfolio—reflecting the classic photo edition box—and, second, as exhibition prints in two different sizes: the large format is reserved for the sectional image showing the veranda with the black door opening and the interiors with a white window, while a smaller format was chosen for the objects shown in close-up. The large-format pictures are printed in "archival pigment print" on matte-luster Museo Silver Rag Paper, which was perfected for black-and-white photographs. The density of the print and the rich, wide-ranging tonal values give the darkness of the door opening a virtually palpable depth and substance, while the gray shades in the shadows, the grain in the wood surfaces, and the worn, scratched surfaces of the aluminum cutlery, range from dark gray to silver. For the smaller exhibition prints, Oskar Schmidt chose to use the gelatin silver printing technique, which he carried out himself in his own laboratory (that is, they were created in the darkroom and not, like the larger-format pictures, as digital inkjet prints). This is another classic processing technique; one which gives black-and-white photographs a slight sepia tone, but without reducing the diversity of the gray, silver, and metallic nuances.

Based upon the historic black-and-white photographs of the Burroughs family by Walker Evans from 1936 Oskar Schmidt reconstructed the wooden house of the Burroughs family in his studio. With an analog large-format camera, the artist provides himself with a minimalist setting: variations featuring objects in front of and within the black doorway on the veranda; close-up shots of objects; interior scenes arranged around a bright, white window.

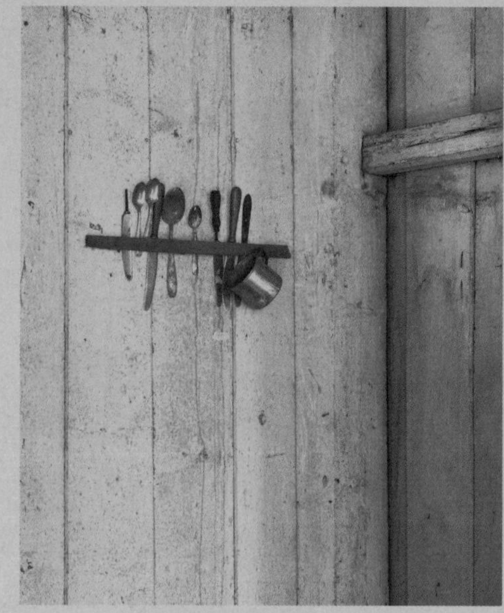

Oskar Schmidt, *Kitchen Wall,* 2011

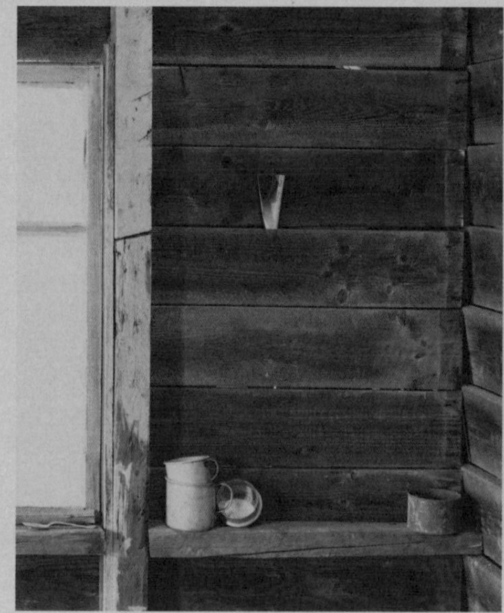

Oskar Schmidt, *Picture,* 2013

The Dramaturgy of Objects

The initial fascination one feels in viewing Oskar Schmidt's photography comes from his apparent repetition of the same motif combined with extremely distinct non-narrative detailing: light and darkness, shades and tones that have an appearance of color, textures and surfaces, emptiness and material substantiality. In this extremely reduced dramatic arena, objects play the role of actors that are non-moving and yet moving—they could be described as traces of imagined lives that have sunk from view in the darkness of history. The constellation of objects that appear several times in different parts of the pictures represents a kind of "family of objects." A wooden ladder and a chair occupy the empty spaces left by the parents, and the small cooking utensils, the cans, and paper bags, can be read as the horde of children of former times, posed by the photographer in front of the camera alone or in groups of two or three. The longer one looks, the more one

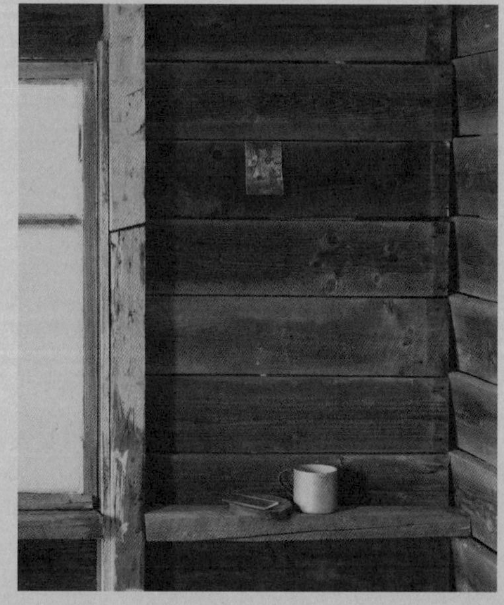

Oskar Schmidt, *Picture (No. 2),* 2013

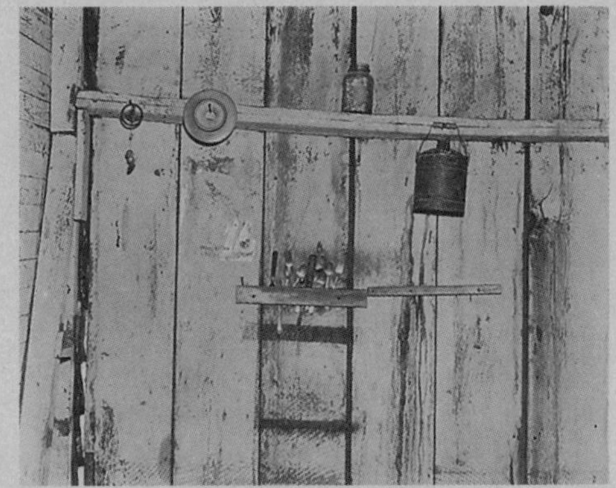

Walker Evans, *Kitchen Wall in Bud Fields' House, Hale County, Alabama*, 1936

und dingliche Präsenz. Die Objekte spielen in diesem äußerst reduzierten Bühnenraum die Rolle unbewegt-bewegter Darsteller, gleichsam Signaturen eines imaginierten, in das Dunkel der Historie abgetauchten Lebens. Die Konstellation der Objekte, die in unterschiedlichen Nachbarschaften und mehrfach auftreten, repräsentiert so etwas wie eine „Familie der Dinge". Eine hölzerne Leiter und ein Stuhl besetzen die Leerstelle der Eltern, die kleinteiligen Kochgeschirre, Kannen, Papiertüten nehmen den Platz der in früherer Zeit üblichen großen Kinderschar ein, die der Fotograf allein, zu zweit oder zu dritt vor der Kamera posieren lässt. Je länger man schaut, desto mehr entsteht der Eindruck extremer Langzeitbelichtungen, aus denen alles Bewegliche, Lebendige verschwunden ist und nur das Statische vom Kameraauge erfasst werden konnte.

Die Verweigerung des Künstlers, über ein vielteiliges Szenario uns ein „Abbild" einer komplexen historischen / gesellschaftlichen Situation zu vermitteln, befreit und stimuliert unmittelbar die Imagination. Was dokumentieren, was bezeugen, was erzählen diese Objekte? Eine nochmals neue Qualität und Intensität gewinnt die Betrachtung der Fotografien, wenn man auf die minimalen inszenatorischen Momente achtet, mit welchen Oskar Schmidt die Schwärze der Türöffnung selbst zum eigentlichen Subjekt der Szene macht: Der schmale Streifen eines Holzbrettes, von innen am Türrahmen befestigt, zieht unseren Blick über die Schwelle in das Innere des Raumes. In anderen Fotos sind es Papiertüte und Geschirr – auf der Schwelle stehend, halb in helles Studiolicht / helles Tageslicht, halb in das Dunkel des Raumes getaucht –, die unsere Aufmerksamkeit in die scheinbar undurchdringliche Schwärze locken. Und erst jetzt erahnen wir auch Details des Innenraumes wie Dachbalken oder die dunkle Struktur der Dielen. Das Schwarz der Türöffnung ist durch diese inszenierten Übergänge gleichsam als nackte Abstraktion aufgehoben und gewinnt eine physische Präsenz. Die schlichte Kargheit der stilllebenhaften Szenarien erfährt durch die Körperlichkeit – man möchte sagen: durch die Sinnlichkeit des Dunkel – eine eigentümliche Vitalität und magisch-surreale Aufladung.

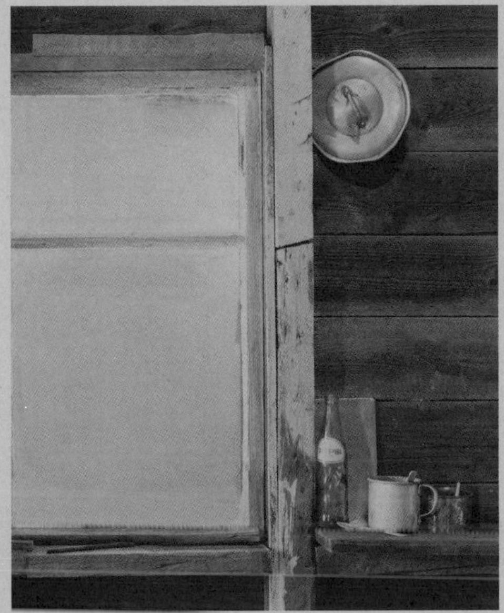

Oskar Schmidt, *Bottle*, 2013

Neben der Porträtaufnahme von Vater und Tochter Burroughs vor der dunklen Türöffnung ihrer Hütte in den Bildern von Evans ist es vor allem eine ungewöhnlich „piktorale", nahezu abstrakt wirkende Aufnahme eines Details der hölzernen Wand im Innenraum, auf welche sich Oskar Schmidt in seiner *The American Series* bezieht: Walker Evans gelingt es mit diesem ganz auf lichte Grauwerte hin konzipierten Stillleben die ökonomisch erzwungene Reduktion des ländlichen Lebens auf einige existenzielle Dinge visuell vor Augen zu führen. Unter den wenigen reinen Interieuraufnahmen, die Evans gemacht hat, hat sich Oskar Schmidt ohne Zweifel mit dem Foto der *Kitchen Wall* eine der am stärksten ästhetisch „komponierten" Aufnahmen ausgewählt. Schmidt destilliert für seine fotografischen Stillleben noch einmal einzelne Objekte aus der Vorlage heraus, die auf alle erzählerischen Momente zugunsten eines piktoralen Minimalismus verzichten.

In den neueren Fotografien von Schmidts *The American Series* korrespondiert mit dem dunklen Türdurchgang der 2011/12 entstandenen Bilder das hell überstrahlte Weiß eines Fensters im Innenraum der Hütte, das – ebenso wie das Schwarz der Türöffnung – den Blick hinaus aus dem Raum zunächst verweigert. Die voyeuristische Neugier des Betrachters zurückweisend, welcher versucht, den historischen / urbanen Kontext dieses aus der Zeit gefallenen Interieurs zu verstehen, wird so gleichsam „reflektiert" und auf sich selbst zurückverwiesen. Auch hier liest man im Nebeneinander der Fotografien auf der Ausstellungswand bzw. im Buch Oskar Schmidts Fensterbilder – ähnlich wie die Serien von Sherrie Levine –

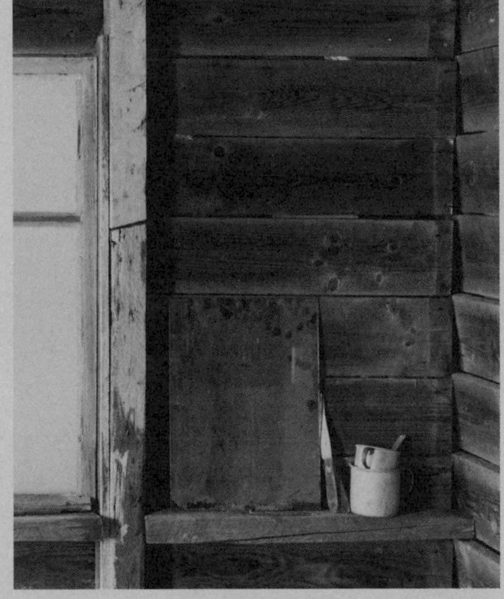

Oskar Schmidt, *Mirror*, 2013

has the impression of an extremely long exposure time: everything mobile and living has vanished, so that only static objects remain to be captured by the eye of the camera.

The artist's refusal to convey to us a "likeness," a "facsimile," of a complex historical / social situation through the medium of a scenario in multiple parts liberates and stimulates the imagination in a more direct way. What do these objects document? What do they bear witness to? What do they tell us? The experience of viewing the photos gains a new quality and intensity when one becomes aware of the minimalist factors in their composition. Oskar Schmidt makes the blackness of the doorway itself the main subject of the scene: the narrow stripe of a wooden board which is secured to the door frame from the inside draws our gaze over the threshold and into the space's interior. In some of his other photos, it is paper bags and items of crockery—standing on the threshold, half in the bright studio light / the bright daylight and half submerged in the darkness of the room—that draw our attention into the seemingly impenetrable blackness. Only then do we recognize other details of the interior space, such as the roof beams and the dark structure of the boards. These choreographed transitions lift the blackness of the doorway, metaphorically speaking, into the realms of bare abstraction, so that it gains a physical presence. The physicality—one might say the sensuality—of the darkness gives the plain severity of these still-life scenes a curious vitality, and a magical / surreal charge.

In addition to the portrait photograph of father and daughter Burroughs in front of the dark doorway of their cabin in the images by Evans, Oskar Schmidt refers in his *The American Series* to a particularly unusual "pictorial," almost abstract-seeming shot of a detail of the wooden wall in the interior: with this still life conceived completely in sparing gray tones Walker Evans succeeds in showing the rural economic necessity of downgrading to just a few existential things. From among the few purely interior photographs that Evans shot, with the photo *Kitchen Wall* Oskar Schmidt without a doubt chose one of the strongest aesthetically "composed" photographs. For his photographic still lifes Schmidt distilled once again from the originals individual objects that forgo all narrative moments in favor of a pictorial minimalism.

In the more recent photographs from Schmidt's *The American Series,* the white brightness of a window, seen in the interior of the house, corresponds with the dark doorway of the photos made in 2011/12; like the black doorway, the window initially refuses to let the gaze of the viewer pass beyond the space. With the voyeuristic curiosity of the viewer rejected, any attempts to understand the historic / urban context of this out-of-time interior scene is thus "reflected" and referred back to the viewer. Also here one reads Oskar Schmidt's window images in the juxtaposition of the photographs on the exhibition wall or in the book—similar to the series by Sherrie Levine—as a sequence of "self-quotations" or "auto copies," as the first fleeting glance seems to discern a uniform setting, where nevertheless a subtle dramaturgy of objects demands the attention of the viewer.

The model set built by Schmidt in the studio focuses on a section of the wooden wall and floor boards, the window framed by rough beams. The camera seems to circle the window in a small stoic movement, where with the shift of the view the things also change their location. With their appearance and disappearance the paper bag, pot, towel, cup, lid, and tin can "register" a temporal progression in the apparent motionlessness of the still life.

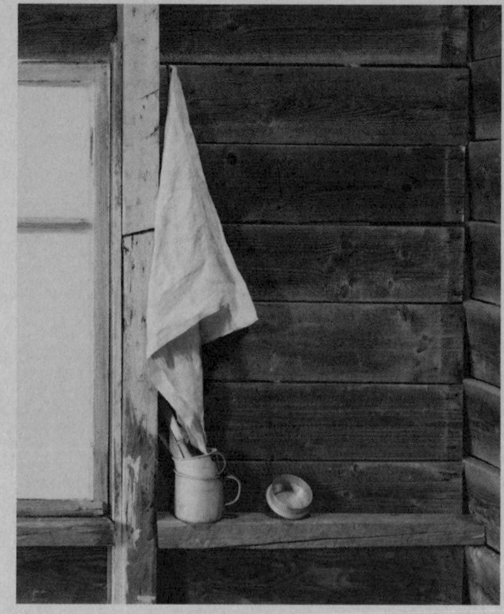

Oskar Schmidt, *Towel,* 2013

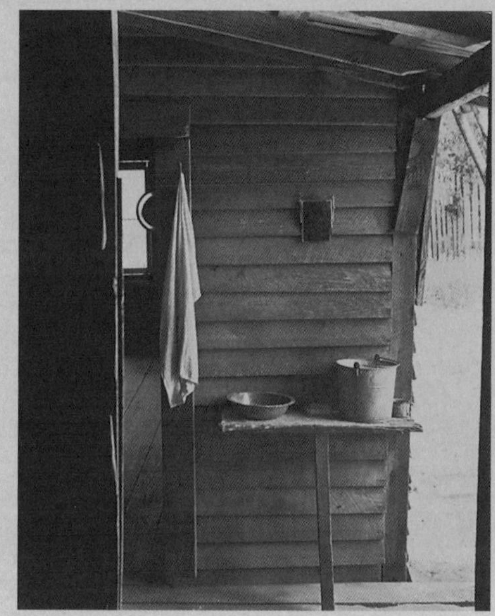

Walker Evans, *Washstand with Pail, Bowl, and Mirror in Dog Run of Burroughs Home, Hale County, Alabama,* 1936

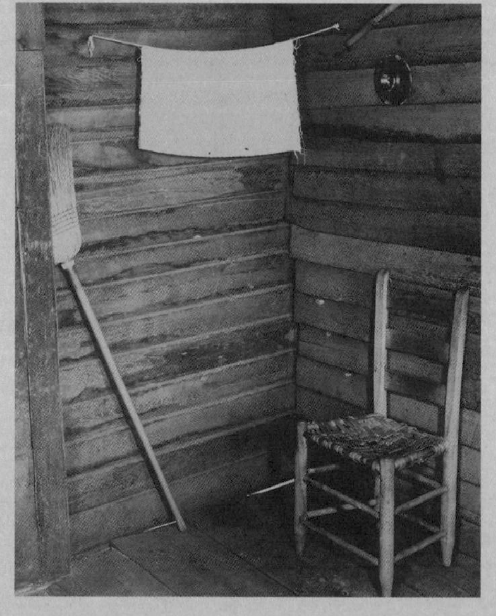

Walker Evans, *Kitchen Corner, Tenant Farmhouse, Hale County, Alabama,* 1936

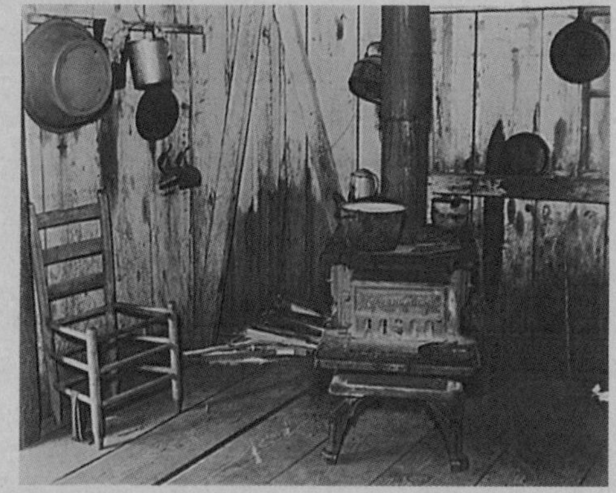

Walker Evans, *Corner of Kitchen in Bud Fields' Home, Hale County, Alabama,* 1935 oder / or 1936

als eine Folge von „Selbstzitaten", von „Auto-Kopien", da der erste flüchtige Blick ein gleichbleibendes Setting zu erkennen meint, wo doch eine subtile Dramaturgie der Objekte die Aufmerksamkeit des Betrachters fordert.

Die von Schmidt im Studio gebaute Modellsituation fokussiert einen Ausschnitt von Bretterwand und Dielenboden, das Fenster ist eingefasst von groben Balken. Die Kamera scheint in einem langsamen, stoischen Lauf das Fenster zu umkreisen, wobei mit der Verschiebung des Ausschnitts auch die Dinge ihren Ort wechseln. Papiertüte, Topf, Tuch, Becher, Deckel und Dose „schreiben" mit ihrem Auftauchen und Verschwinden einen zeitlichen Verlauf in die scheinbare Statik des Stilllebens ein.

Obwohl Oskar Schmidt nicht – wie Levine 1981 in ihrer Arbeit *After Walker Evans* – Bilder von Walker Evans direkt refotografiert, sondern das gebaute Studiomodell zwischen die fotografische Vorlage und das analog aufgenommene Bild stellt, zielen auch seine Fotografien auf eine Theorie der Bilder, in denen Fragen nach Ursprung und Urheber, nach Originalität und Authentizität verhandelt werden. Indem in seinen Werken immer nur auf ein Original verwiesen wird, stellt sich zugleich das Thema der Repräsentation. Oskar Schmidts Wahl einer technisch und formal „traditionell", ja „altmeisterlich" anmutenden Bildsprache ermöglicht es ihm, ein virtuoses Spiel von Original, Zitat, Kopie und Kopie der Kopie zu inszenieren. Am schönsten ist dieses Vexierspiel der „Bilder von Bildern" vielleicht in jenen Fotos der *Windows*-Serie gelungen, in welchen ein blinder Spiegel bzw. kleine, auf die Wand genagelte Bilder auftauchen, deren Motive allerdings kaum zu erkennen bzw. zerrissen sind. In dem blinden Spiegel scheint sich das über Eck hängende weiße Tuch als grauer Schatten zu reflektieren, welches wir aus den Fotos von Evans/Levine kennen – ein letztes Bild nach dem Ende der Bilder zitierend.

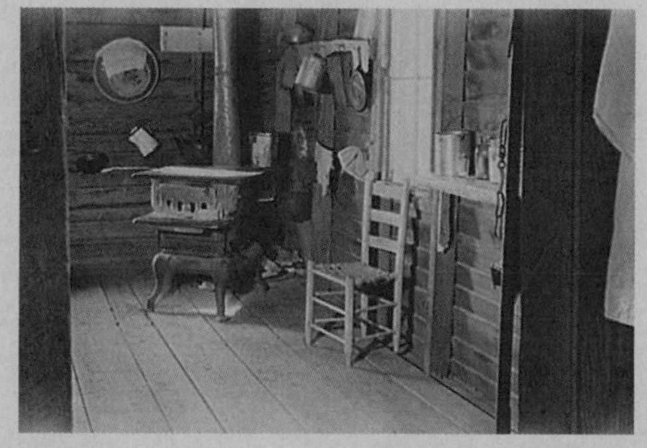

Walker Evans, *Kitchen in Home of Floyd Burroughs, Tenant Farmer, Hale County, Alabama,* 1936

The American Series im Werkzusammenhang

Oskar Schmidt erscheint als ein leidenschaftlicher Regisseur des absoluten, des perfekten Stilllebens als Teil eines aktuell relevanten Themas der Fotografie. „Leidenschaftlich" spricht die Obsession seiner Zuwendung und Ausdeutung des Themas „Stillleben" an, aber auch die scheinbar unbeirrbare Ausdauer, mit welcher er seit rund zehn Jahren wenige Motive und deren punktgenaue Inszenierung mit der Kamera umkreist, einkreist.[4] Das zentrale Schwarz der Tür, das Weiß des Fensters in *The American Series* hat Vorläufer im frühen fotografischen Werk von Oskar Schmidt (*Wiedergängerinnen*, 2005–2009) in Gestalt weniger Möbelobjekte, welche den reduzierten und stilllebenhaft arrangierten Objekten und Personen einen äußerst verknappten Ort, eine minimale Verankerung im Unspezifischen eines Raumausschnitts gaben: Ein alter Küchentisch, auf welchem eine Weltkugel oder Totenkopfzeichnungen liegen oder ein kleines Kartenhaus steht; Stuhl, Tisch, Hocker, auch sie eine museale Welt der einfachen Dinge repräsentierend, die einen Sockel hergeben für die objekthafte Inszenierung junger Mädchen mit Shirt, Rock und weißen Strümpfen. Bezüge zu Ikonen der Malereigeschichte gibt es vielfältig in den früheren Fotografien: das Kartenhäuschen von Chardin, die Stillleben mit Totenschädeln eines Cézanne, und eben die artifiziellen Körperhaltungen junger Mädchen in den Gemälden von Balthus.

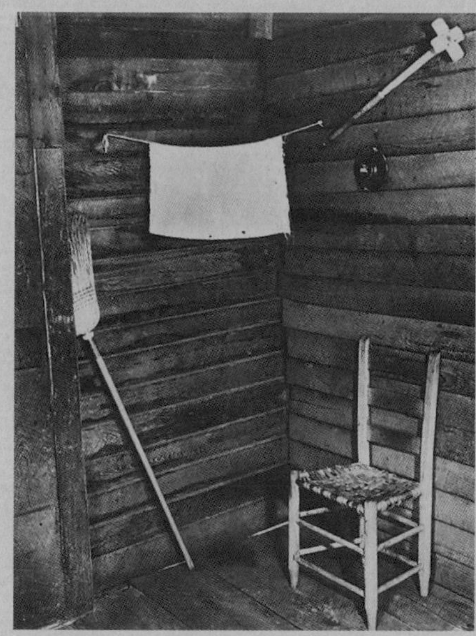

Sherrie Levine, *After Walker Evans: 7,* 1981

In der 2010 entstandenen Serie *Interieurs* ist es dann das Licht selbst, das zum Akteur und Darsteller in Korrespondenz zu und im Zwiegespräch mit jenen abgestoßenen, alten Möbeln der früheren Serie wird. Zwei niedrig liegende, selbst nicht sichtbare Fenster reflektieren sich als lichte bzw. diffuse hellere Flächen auf der Wand eines ansonsten dunklen Raumes, ihre Lichtbahnen vermit-

Although Oskar Schmidt does not directly re-photograph the images of Walker Evans—like Levine in 1981 in her work *After Walker Evans*—but rather positions the built studio model between the photographic original and the image captured via analog means, his photographs also aim towards a theory of images that deals with questions of source and author as well as originality and authenticity. Since there is always just one original that is referenced in his works, he takes on the theme of representation at the same time. Oskar Schmidt's choice of a visual language that is technically and formally "traditional" and indeed not unlike the "Old Masters" makes it possible for him to stage a virtuoso play on original, quotation, copy, and copy of the copy. This deceptive game of "pictures of pictures" is most successfully apparent in the photos of the *Windows* series in which a clouded mirror or small pictures nailed to the wall appear, with motifs that are unrecognizable or torn. In the clouded mirror the white cloth hanging in the corner seems to be reflected as a gray shadow, which we know from the photos of Evans/Levine—a final image after the end of images is quoted.

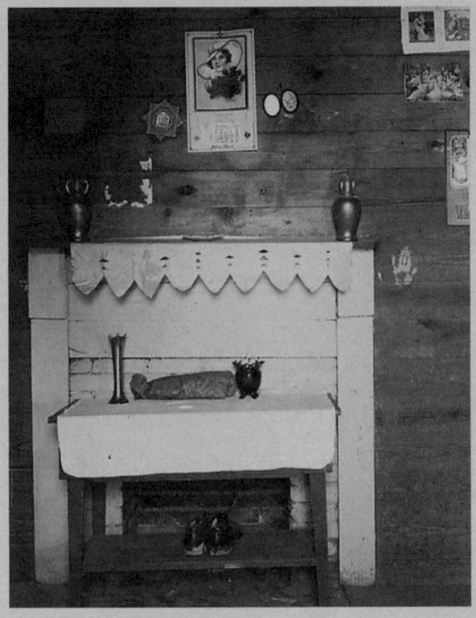

Walker Evans, *Table, Fireplace, and Pictures on Wall of Floyd Burroughs's Bedroom, Hale County, Alabama*, 1936

The American Series in the Context of the Artist's Oeuvre

Oskar Schmidt appears as a passionate choreographer of the absolute, of the perfect still life as part of a highly current and relevant theme in photography. The "obsessive" character of the way in which he applies himself to and interprets the theme of "the still life" is passionate. Equally passionate is the seemingly unerring perseverance with which he has, for the past ten years, pursued and zeroed in on a small number of motifs with his camera, perfecting their choreography.[4] The central, black shape of the doorway and the whiteness of the window in *The American Series* are prefigured in previous photographic works by Oskar Schmidt (such as *Wiedergängerinnen,* 2005–2009) in the form of a few articles of furniture, which gave the still-life arrangements of objects and the people an exceptionally truncated sense of specific location, a minimal anchoring in an excerpted space that is highly non-specific in character: an old kitchen table upon which a globe, a picture of a skull, or a small house of cards stands, or a chair, a table, or a stool (which, in themselves, represent a museum-like world of simple things) providing pedestals upon which young girls in shirts, skirts, and white stockings are presented like objects. References to icons of painting history are myriad in Schmidt's early early photographs: the house of cards of Chardin, the still lifes with skulls of Cézanne, and even the artificial postures of the young girls in the paintings of Balthus.

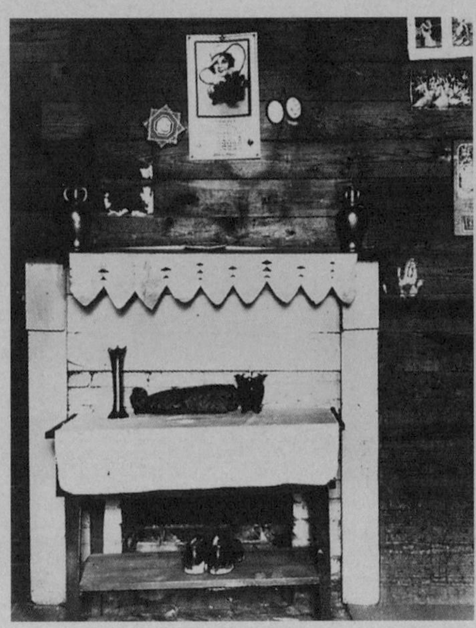

Sherrie Levine, *After Walker Evans: 8*, 1981

In the series *Interieurs,* created in 2010, it is the light itself that becomes actor and performer; the light corresponds with and enters into a dialogue with the battered old furniture seen in the previous series. Two low-set windows (not themselves visible) are reflected by the lighter colored or diffuse lighter surfaces we can see on the wall of an otherwise dark room. The streaks of light cause the isolated objects—a chair, a kneeler, a stool, a bowl—to cast dramatic shadows. Schmidt explores the power a pattern of light has to transform a scene—something that we know from the paintings of Willem Claesz. Heda and the landscape photography of Ansel Adams. In the *Interieur* series, however, light remains an object, and an object of photographic research. It is only with the photographs of the *The American Series* that the character of light and darkness is heightened, so that it becomes a physical and a subjective presence. Painterly, atmospheric moments coalesce in Schmidt's photographs with aspects of the "sculptural" staging of his built interiors and with a decidedly analytical/conceptual approach.

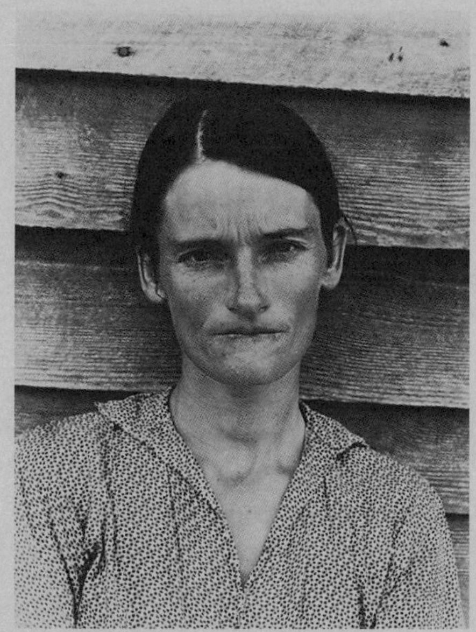

Sherrie Levine, *After Walker Evans: 4*, 1981

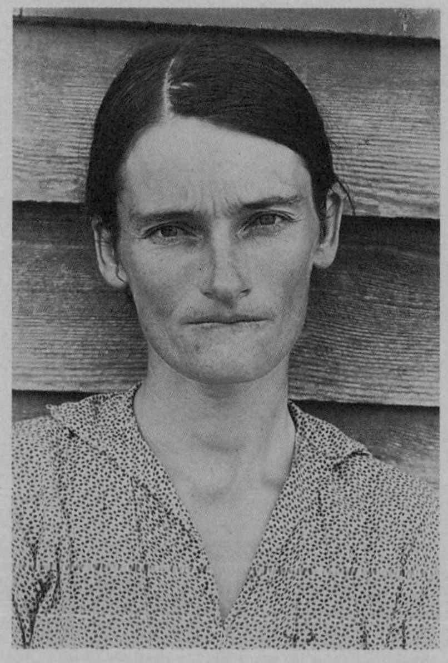

Walker Evans, *Alabama Tenant Farmer Wife*, 1936

teln den alleinstehenden Objekten – ein Stuhl, eine Kniebank, ein Hocker, eine Schüssel – einen dramatischen Schattenwurf. Schmidt spielt in dieser Serie die szenische Verwandlungskraft einer Lichtregie durch, wie man sie aus Bildern von Willem Claesz. Heda bis zu den Landschaftsfotos eines Ansel Adams kennt. Trotzdem: Das Licht bleibt in der *Interieur*-Serie ein Gegenstand, ein Objekt der fotografischen Recherche, und erst die Bilder der *The American Series* steigern dann das Wesen von Licht und Dunkel zu einer physisch-subjekthaften Präsenz. Malerische, atmosphärische Momente verbinden sich in Schmidts Fotografien mit Aspekten einer „skulpturalen" Inszenierung seiner gebauten Interieurs sowie mit einer dezidiert analytisch-konzeptuellen Herangehensweise.

Die Vorbilder: Walker Evans & James Agee, Sherrie Levine

„Zwei Fotografien aus Walker Evans Serien sind es vor allem, die die Grundlage meiner Bilder *The American Series* darstellen: der Familienvater Burroughs, gemeinsam mit einer der Töchter vor der dunklen Öffnung der Tür seiner Hütte sitzend, und eine Interieuraufnahme der Hütte ohne Menschen. Meine Bilder sind zum Teil ‚Bilder über Bilder', sie stehen aber auch für sich selbst. In meinem Atelier habe ich in Lebensgröße diese Situation nachgebaut und dann darin meine Bilder inszeniert. Der zum Teil hohe inszenatorisch-ästhetische Eingriff von Evans in seinen exemplarisch gewordenen sozialdokumentarischen Fotografien[5] zeigt für mich sehr deutlich das hohe Konstruktionspotenzial der Fotografie an sich. Für mein Bild *Kitchen Wall* gibt es ebenfalls eine Vorlage von Walker Evans, die ich zitiere, jedoch nehme ich nur das Detail des Bildes bzw. den Ausschnitt mit dem provisorisch an der Wand angebrachten Essbesteck, der dann bei mir zum vollständigen Bild wird. Anders als Sherrie Levine refotografiere ich nicht direkt die Bilder von Walker Evans. Es findet immer eine Transformation der Bildwiederholung statt. Zudem interessieren mich vor allem die stilllebenhaften Momente in den Bildern. Also die fast minimalistische Inszenierung des Raumes und der wenigen darin befindlichen Objekte, wie eine Schüssel oder ein Topf. Die starke Reduktion auf die Objekthaftigkeit und die Form der einfachsten Dinge beschäftigen mich."[6]

Auf den fotohistorisch und sozialgeschichtlich bedeutenden Hintergrund von Schmidts *The American Series* ist Bettina Gockel 2012 ausführlich eingegangen.[7] 1935 rief die US-amerikanische Regierung das Projekt „Farm Security Administration" ins Leben, um in der Zeit der Great Depression und des New Deal die Farmer in den Südstaaten zu unterstützen, die zum Teil katastrophalen Lebensumstände zu dokumentieren und in den reicheren Bundesstaaten um Hilfe zu werben. Verbunden damit war ein legendär gewordenes Programm mit Aufträgen für Fotodokumentationen an Fotografen wie Walker Evans, Dorothea Lange und Gordon Parks. Evans aber – seiner künstlerischen Maxime „No Politics" folgend – stieg schon nach etwa einem Jahr wieder aus und nahm stattdessen 1936 einen Auftrag des Magazins Fortune an, gemeinsam mit dem Schriftsteller James Agee drei Pächter-Familien in Alabama, darunter die Familie Burroughs, zu porträtieren. Die Fotos – sie zeigen die Familie in Einzelporträts oder kleinen Gruppen im Umfeld ihrer kargen Holzhütte, begleitet auch von Evans leicht inszenierten Szenen des leeren Wohnraums – wurden zum Symbol für die Armut im ländlichen Süden. Der ästhetisch neue und herausragende Aspekt der Aufnahmen von Evans lässt sich benennen mit den Momenten von Reduktion und Inszenierung: Die Kamera geht ganz nah an die Gesichter heran und blendet das Umfeld aus, sie liest den Physiognomien selbst das Drückende und Auszehrende der Zeit ab, ohne doch den Menschen ihre Individualität und Würde zu nehmen. Zugleich findet so etwas wie

The Inspirations: Walker Evans & James Agee, Sherrie Levine

"Two photographs from Walker Evans's series in particular provided the foundation for my *The American Series* pictures: Burroughs, the father, sitting in front of the doorway opening of his hut with one of his daughters, and an interior shot of the hut, with no people present. My pictures are to some extent 'pictures about pictures,' but they also exist in their own right. In my studio, I reconstructed this situation to scale and then staged my pictures within it. I feel that Evans's sometimes quite extensive compositional and aesthetic intervention in his social documentary pictures (which have come to be seen as typical of the social documentary genre) shows the constructive potential of photography itself. My picture *Kitchen Wall* is also based on a photograph by Walker Evans. I quote his picture, but only a single detail from it—the section that contains eating utensils arranged against the wall in a makeshift way, which I turn into a self-contained picture. Unlike Sherrie Levine, I do not directly appropriate the pictures of Walker Evans. I always transform the pictures that I revisit. In addition to this, it is the still-life factors of the pictures that interest me the most—the almost minimalist presentation of the space and of the few objects within it, such as a bowl or a pot. I am concerned with a process of extreme reduction that leaves only the pure 'object' character—and with the shapes of the most simple things."[5]

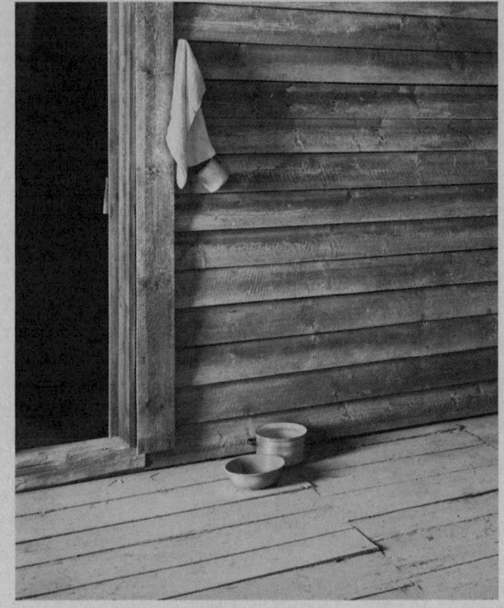

Oskar Schmidt, *Cookware and Towel*, 2011

Bettina Gockel discussed in detail the photo- and social-historical significance behind Schmidt's *The American Series* in 2012.[6] In 1935 the U.S. government created the Farm Security Administration to support the farmers in the South, to document what were in part catastrophic living conditions, and to attract aid from the wealthier states. This was linked to a program of commissioned photography, now legendary, where photographers such as Walker Evans, Dorothea Lange, and Gordon Parks created documentary photography. However, Evans left the project approximately a year later, in line with his artistic philosophy of "No Politics." In 1936, he accepted an alternative commission from the magazine *Fortune* to collaborate with author James Agee in creating portraits of three Alabama sharecropper families, among them the Burroughs. The photographs—individual or small group portraits showing the family in the environs of their bare wooden hut, accompanied by Evans's somewhat staged scenes of the empty living space—became a symbol of poverty in the rural South. The aesthetically new and exceptional factor in Evans's photographs lies in their reduction and in presenting the faces in close-up, excluding the surroundings and reading oppression and deprivation in the subjects' physiognomy without destroying the individuality and dignity of these people. In addition, a form of picture editing takes place in front of the camera: Evans positioned the members of the family within the narrow confines of their veranda. He also altered the interior of their poor home according to photographic and aesthetic criteria, thereby giving the photographs a timeless quality that goes far beyond social reporting.[7]

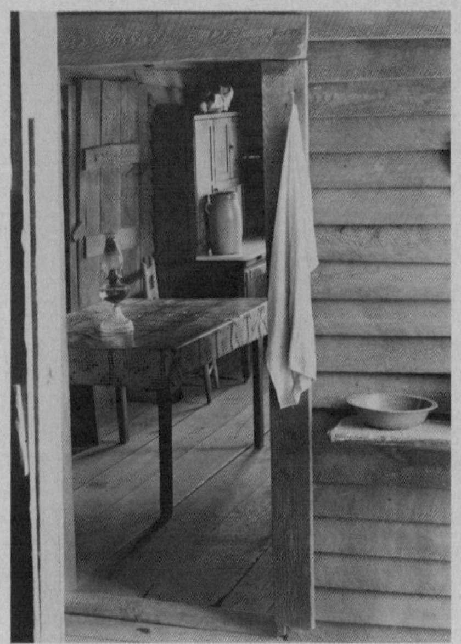

Walker Evans, *Washstand with View Into Dining Area of Burroughs's Home, Hale County, Alabama*, 1936

Fortune, however, later decided not to publish the Evans/Agee report, which had turned out to be too long. Agee published it in book form in 1941.[8] By moving beyond traditional forms of documentary journalism, Evans/Agee succeeded in laying the foundations for a documentary literature form, combining reported facts with literary and visual complexity, and with a quality of poetic beauty.

The background for the multimedia work by Sherrie Levine (born 1947, lives in New York) can be briefly sketched as follows: an early recognition that the experience of art is initially controlled by the medium of photographic reproduction; Conceptual art of the 1960s; the discussions in the 1970s on feminism and

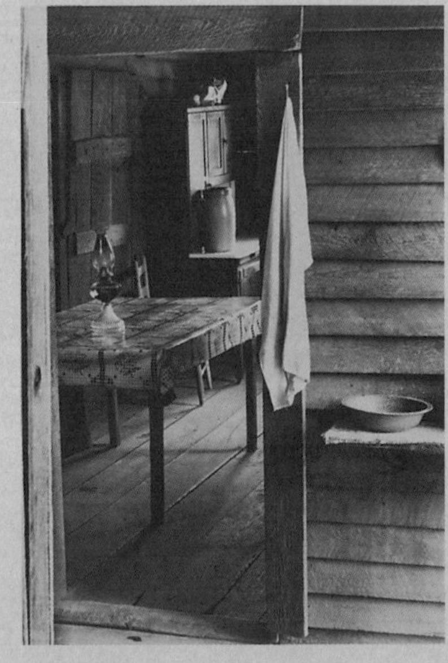

Sherrie Levine, *After Walker Evans: 11*, 1981

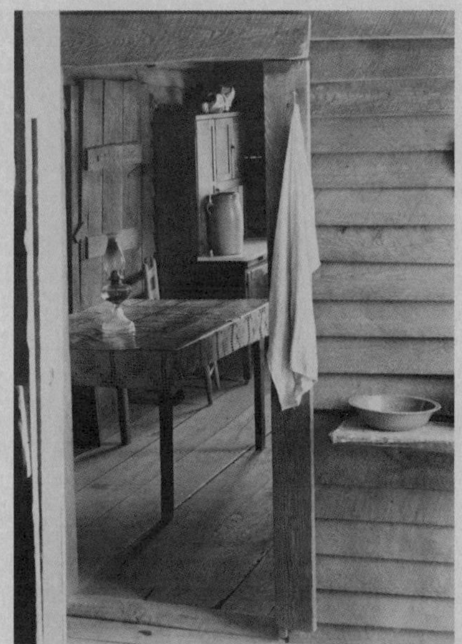

Michael Mandiberg, *Untitled (AfterSherrieLevine.com/6.jpg), 3250px × 4250px (at 850dpi)*, 2001

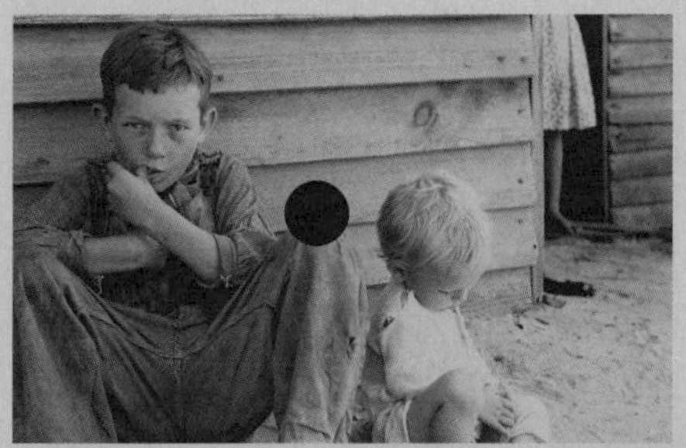

Lisa Oppenheim, *Killed Negatives: After Walker Evans*, 2007–2009

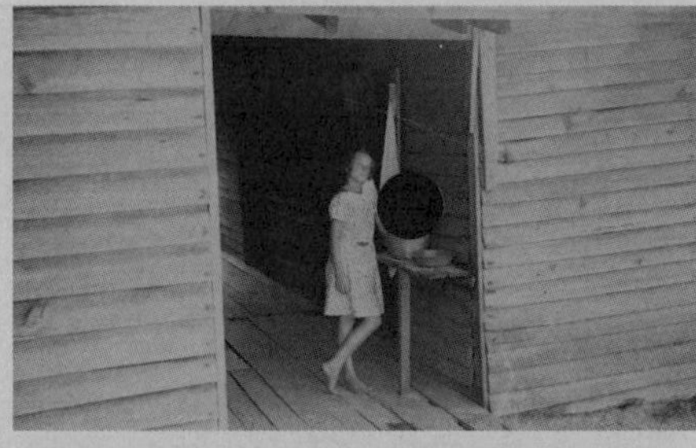

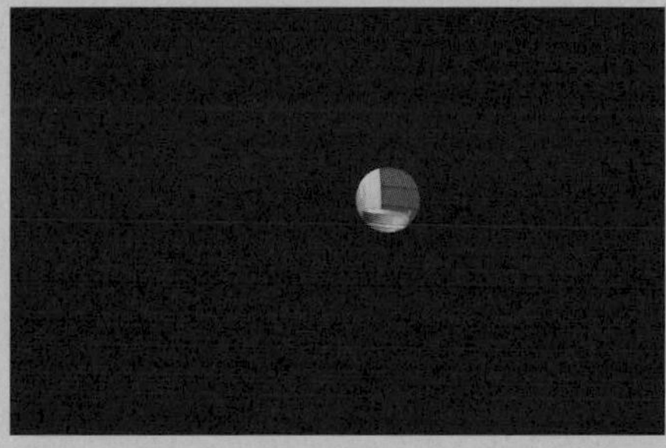

Lisa Oppenheim, *Killed Negatives: After Walker Evans*, 2007–2009

Bildbearbeitung vor der Kamera statt: Evans arrangierte die Mitglieder der Familie im engen Umfeld ihrer Veranda und veränderte auch das Innere ihrer ärmlichen Wohnung nach fotografisch-ästhetischen Gesichtspunkten. So gewinnen die Fotos eine Zeitlosigkeit, die weit über den Anlass einer Sozialreportage hinausgeht.

Fortune veröffentlichte den gemeinsamen, zu lang geratenen Bericht von Evans/Agee dann doch nicht, sodass Agee diesen 1941 als Buch herausbrachte.[8] Traditionelle Formen eines dokumentarischen Journalismus hinter sich lassend, gelang Evans/Agee die Grundlegung einer dokumentarischen Literaturform, die den Tatsachenbericht mit literarisch-visueller Komplexität und Momenten poetischer Schönheit verbindet.

Der Hintergrund für das multimediale Werk von Sherrie Levine (geb. 1947, lebt in New York) kann knapp etwa so skizziert werden: die frühe Erkenntnis, dass Kunsterfahrung zunächst über das Medium fotografischer Reproduktionen gesteuert wird; die Conceptual Art der 1960er Jahre; die Diskussionen der 1970er Jahre zu Feminismus und Ökonomiekritik; die kunstkritischen Diskurse um Originalität, Autorschaft und Tauschwert. *After Walker Evans* war die zweite Fotoserie, mit welcher die Künstlerin 1981 in der New Yorker Galerie Metro Pictures auftrat und die Appropriation Art mitbegründete. Aus hunderten von Schwarz-Weiß-Aufnahmen, von Evans zwischen 1935 und 1938 fotografiert, hatte Levine 22 Motive für ihre erste, viel diskutierte Einzelausstellung ausgewählt und direkt aus der Publikation von 1941 refotografiert. Es sind jene Motive, welche – einzeln wie in der seriellen Zusammenfassung – die unheimliche Traurigkeit von Evans Blick auf seine Zeit noch einmal verdichten: Porträts der Familie Burroughs vor ihrer Hütte, Fassaden einfacher Landkirchen, primitiv ausgehobene Grabstellen im Nirgendwo einer Sandfläche.

Sherrie Levine hatte von Beginn konzeptuell an eine Fortführung dieser Serie im Sinne des Selbstzitats, der „Auto-Kopie" gedacht, die jedoch erst ab 1990 entstand: *Untitled (After Walker Evans Negative).* Noch einmal 22 Fotos, von ihren eigenen schwarz-weißen Fotos nach Evans auf Umkehrpapier gedruckt, sodass jenes in die Raumecke der Burrough'schen Holzhütte gespannte weiße Tuch, wie Evans und Levine nach Evans es festgehalten hatten, plötzlich schwarz hervortritt, die Schatten weiß werden und die hellen Fensteröffnungen schwarz wie die Türöffnung in den Bildern von Oskar Schmidt.

Dieser Serie von Levine's *Negatives* gehen weitere Bearbeitungen parallel, in welchen die Künstlerin mit Techniken, Materialien und Formaten spielt: Fotogravure auf koloriertem Papier, Umkehrdrucke der *Negatives* in der Serie von Silbergelatineprints *Untitled (After Walker Evans Positive),* montiert auf Holz, schließlich 2009 noch einmal eine Serie von *Negatives,* die nun aber durch Digitalisierung von Archivdaten entstehen, also nicht mehr durch Abfotografieren von Evans' bzw. eigener Aufnahmen.[9]

„Ich glaube", hat Levine 1986 in Anspielung auf Samuel Becketts Theaterstück *Endspiel* formuliert, „dass es in der Moderne eine lange Tradition von Endspielkunst gibt, angefangen mit Dada und den Suprematisten (wenn man so will), und jede Menge Künstler haben schon das letzte Bild gemalt. Viele von uns haben Spaß daran, sich in einem Niemandsland zu bewegen. Was zählt ist, nicht den Humor zu verlieren; es ist ja am Ende nur Kunst."[11]

Die Kette der Kopien und Zitate nach Evans/Levine ist bis in die Gegenwart nicht abgerissen: 2001 hat Michael Mandiberg die Fotografien von Evans/Levine noch einmal als Netzprojekt rekonzeptualisiert. Konkret hat der Künstler die Levine-Serie aus der Sammlung des Metropolitan Museum of Art mit hochauf-

economic criticism; the art critical discourse around originality, authorship, and exchange value. *After Walker Evans* was the second photo series with which the artist emerged in 1981 in New York at Metro Pictures Gallery, cofounding Appropriation art. Out of hundreds of black-and-white images photographed by Evans between 1935 and 1938, Levine had chosen 22 motifs for her first, much discussed solo show, re-photographed directly from the 1941 publication. It is these motifs, which—individually and together—intensify anew the incredible sorrow of Evans's perspective on his time: portraits of the Burroughs family in front of their cabin, façades of simple country churches, primitively dug graves in a sandy nowhere land.

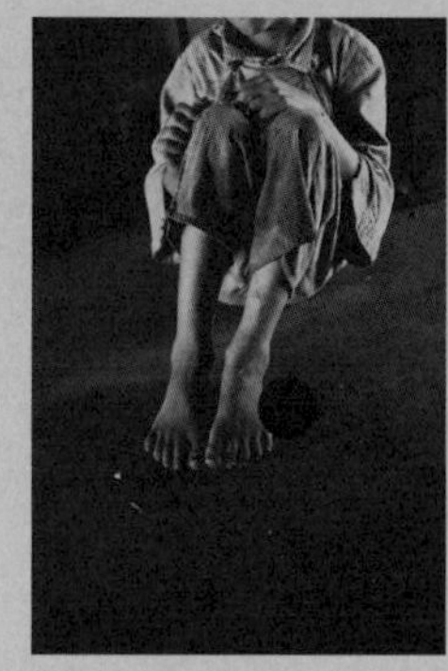

Lisa Oppenheim, *Killed Negatives: After Walker Evans (Small Foot)*, 2009

From the beginning Sherrie Levine had conceptually planned on continuing this series in terms of a self-quotation, the "auto copy," which was, however, created only in 1990: *Untitled (After Walker Evans Negative).* Once again 22 photos after her own black-and-white photos after Evans, printed on silver halide paper, so that the white cloth spanning the corner of the Burroughs family log cabin, as Evans and Levine after Evans captured it, suddenly stands out as black, the shadows become white and the bright window openings as black as the doorway in the images of Oskar Schmidt.

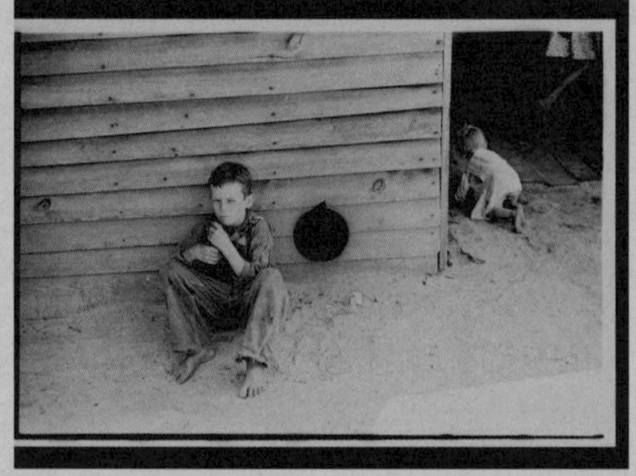

William E. Jones, *Punctured*, 2010; Digitale Bildfolge, s/w, ohne Ton, 4:56 Minuten / sequence of digital files, b/w, mute, 4:56 minutes

Running parallel with this series of Levine's *Negatives* are other adaptations in which the artist plays with techniques, materials, and formats: photogravure on colored paper, reverse printing of the *Negatives* in the gelatin silver print series *Untitled (After Walker Evans Positive)* mounted on wood, ultimately another series of *Negatives* in 2009, that are, however, now created through the digitizing of archived data, and thus no longer through photographing Evans's, or her own photographs.[9]

"I think there is a long modernist tradition of endgame art," stated Levine in 1986 in an allusion to Samuel Beckett's play Endgame, "starting with Dada and the Suprematists (if you like), and a lot of artists have made the last painting ever to be made. It's a no-man's land that a lot of us enjoy moving around in, and the thing is not to lose your sense of humor, because it's only art."[11]

Up to the present time the chain of copies and quotations after Evans/Levine has not been broken: in 2001 Michael Mandiberg reconceptualized again the photographs of Evans/Levine as an online project. Specifically, the artist placed high-resolution images (850 dpi) of the Levine series from the collection of the Metropolitan Museum of Art on the Internet; users of his site can download the images in original size, along with a certificate which attests to the "authenticity" of the Mandiberg photographs.[12]

In 2007, the American artist Lisa Oppenheim selected negatives from the Walker Evans Archive in the Library of Congress, which the director of the Farm Security Administration, Roy Stryker or even Evans himself, had voided by punching holes through the negatives so that they would not be published. What results is a photo series of fragmented positive and negative prints.

William Jones also refers back to the negatives of various photographers of the Farm Security Administration voided by Roy Stryker in a 2010 project in which the negatives are transferred to five-minute loops. This small digression may serve to illustrate that the *The American Series* by Oskar Schmidt is a part of an ongoing look back at Walker Evans by means of diverse media: his work is subject to a new reading and significance in its political gravity and in its formal aesthetic qualities.

gelösten Daten (850 dpi) ins Netz gestellt, User seiner Seite können sich Bilder in Originalgröße herunterladen, zusammen mit einem Zertifikat, welches die „Echtheit" der Mandiberg-Fotos bestätigt.[12]

2007 hat die amerikanische Künstlerin Lisa Oppenheim aus dem Archiv Walker Evans in der Library of Congress Negative ausgewählt, die der staatliche Leiter des Farm Security Projects, Roy Stryker, oder auch Evans selbst durch Stanzen eines kleinen Lochs in das Negativ ungültig gemacht hatten und die nicht publiziert werden sollten. Entstanden ist eine Fotoserie von ausschnitthaften Positiv-/ Negativabzügen.

Auf die von Roy Stryker ungültig gemachten Negative verschiedener Fotografen des Farm Security Projects hat 2010 auch William Jones zurückgegriffen und die Negative in 5-minütige Videoloops übertragen. Man sieht – dazu mag dieser kleine Exkurs hier dienen – dass die *The American Series* von Oskar Schmidt Teil eines medial vielfältigen, aktuellen Blicks zurück auf Walker Evans ist: sein Werk wird in seinem politischen Ernst wie in seinen formal-ästhetischen Qualitäten einer neuen Lektüre und Deutung unterzogen.

Dinglicher Existenzialismus

Wenn man den vorliegenden Text über *The American Series* von Oskar Schmidt noch einmal rasch überliest, treten bestimmte Begrifflichkeiten als charakteristisch hervor: Wiederholung, Nachbild, Bühne, Langzeitbelichtung, Modellhaftigkeit, Dramaturgie der Objekte, Eliminierung des Menschen, Licht und Schatten, Inszenierung, Kargheit, Poesie der minimalen Variation. Von hier ist es dann nicht weit zu Assoziationen an die Prosa und die Dramen eines Samuel Beckett, vor allem aber auch an seine frühen, zum Teil in Stuttgart entstandenen Filme. Schon für Becketts überwältigend radikalen Filme der 1960er Jahre gilt, was kennzeichnend für alle seine Fernsehproduktionen werden sollte: Bewegung und Sprache der Figuren sind gleichsam eingeschlossen in das graue Rechteck des Spielfeldes, welches ein Echo im Fernsehformat findet. Geometrische Grundformen – Lichtfelder als Kreise und Quadrate, Raumecken und Raumöffnungen, in schwarzes Dunkel sich öffnende Fenster und Türen, quadratische oder diagonale Bewegungsbahnen der Figuren – strukturieren und rhythmisieren die minimalisierten Handlungsfragmente.[13] Beckett kultiviert eine Dramaturgie der Objekte und des Lichtes, der Kargheit, er setzt Licht als Dunkel ein und Dunkel als Licht, wenige Accessoires formulieren auf leerer Bühne einen dinghaften Existenzialismus, der die Personen in die Imagination verdrängt. Beckett mag nicht, wie Evans, ein unmittelbares Vorbild für Oskar Schmidt gewesen sein, aber von Beckett her liest man seine Fotografien noch einmal in einem anderen, essenzielleren Licht.

1 Sherrie Levine, in: *Mannerism: A Theory of Culture,* Vancouver Art Gallery 1982, S. 48.

2 Rosalind Krauss, „Die Originalität der Avantgarde", in: *October* (Cambridge, Mass.), 18, Herbst 1981, S. 47–66. Zit. nach Charles Harrison, Paul Wood, „Kunsttheorie im 20. Jahrhundert", Bd. II, Ostfildern 2003, S. 1321.

3 Vgl. „The Pictures Generation, 1974–1984", Ausst.-Kat. The Metropolitan Museum of Art, New York 2009.

4 Wenn man darüber nachdenkt, wie die Serien der reduzierten fotografischen Stillleben von Oskar Schmidt im Feld der zeitgenössischen Kunst zu verorten wären, muss man zunächst an seine frühe malerische Ausbildung erinnern. Die Tradition einer (surreal inszenierenden, fabulierenden) Malerei der älteren Leipziger Schule, vor allem aber auch die jüngeren Entwicklungen der sogenannten Neuen Leipziger Schule (seit 2003 repräsentiert durch Künstler wie Thilo Baumgärtel, Tim Eitel und Martin Weischer) hat Schmidt früh und bewusst mit seinen Fotoserien hinter sich gelassen. In Leipzig war Schmidt vor allem die Ausbildung bei Timm Rautert wichtig: Rautert hat sich als Fotojournalist wie als Künstler immer wieder mit sozialen Themen befasst, dem parallel gehen konzeptuelle Fotoserien und seine „Bildanalytische Photographie".

Malerische, atmosphärische Momente verbinden sich in Schmidts Fotografien mit Aspekten einer „skulpturalen" Inszenierung seiner gebauten Interieurs sowie mit einer dezidiert analytisch-konzeptuellen Herangehensweise – und bringen ihn damit in die Nähe zum Werk von Thomas Demand. Dieser ist in den 1990er Jahren bekannt geworden mit, ausgehend von Fotos, dem 1:1 Nachbau geschichtsträchtiger Orte, Räume oder stilllebenhaft arrangierter Objekte, die dann – unter Weglassung von Details, Schrift, Menschen etc. – so abfotografiert werden, dass gleichsam abstrakte Historienbilder entstehen, die zugleich eine extreme Verdichtung von Erinnerung repräsentieren.

„Retrofotografie" – unter diesem Titel hat jüngst Andreas Müller-Pohle rund zwanzig zeitgenössische Fotografen vorgestellt, die für einen aktuellen Trend von „Retro als Rückgriff auf Ästhetiken der Vergangenheit" einstehen. Vgl. Andreas Müller-Pohle (Hg.), „Retrofotografie", in: *European Photographie,* No. 94, Vol. 34, Issue 2, Winter 2013/14. Der Autor verfolgt hier zwei Aspekte, zum einen das Revival der Analogfotografie sowie historischer Techniken wie Camera Obscura und Sofortbildfotografie in ihrer Verbindung mit digitalen Apparaten und Applikationen. Zum anderen werden Fotografen wie Hisaji Hara oder Alexandra Polina vorgestellt, die kunsthistorische Vorbilder wie die Malerei eines Balthus bzw. Bilder der russischen Revolutionskunst reinszenieren.

5 Zu den ästhetisch-inszenatorischen Eingriffen von Walker Evans siehe u. a. http://opinionator.blogs.nytimes.com/2009/10/20/the-case-of-the-inappropriate-alarm-clock-part-3/?_php=true&_type=blogs&_r=0

6 Zitat von Oskar Schmidt an die Verfasserin, September 2013.

7 Bettina Gockel, „Dokumentarisch = Amerikanisch? Zu Oskar Schmidts Fotoserie *The American Series*", in: *Oskar Schmidt – Dust Bowl Years,* Ausst.-Kat. Scheublein + BAK, Zürich 2012.

8 Das Buch erschien unter dem Titel „Let Us Now Praise Famous Men" (dt. zuerst 1989 als „Preisen will ich die großen Männer").

9 Vgl. Johanna Burton, „Not the Last Word. Reflections on Sherrie Levine's *After Walker Evans Negative*", in: *Artforum,* September 2009, S. 264–271 f.

10 Nachweise für alle Fotos Levine und Oppenheim unter http://www.randomradiance.com/2011_01_01_archive.html

11 Sherrie Levine, in: Harrison/Wood 2003 (wie Anm. 3), S. 1346. Originalzitat in: *Flash Art,* 129, Sommer 1986.

12 Siehe die Diskussion des Projekts im Wired Magazine, 2001, http://archive.wired.com/culture/lifestyle/news/2001/05/43902

13 Samuel Beckett, *Hey Joe, Quadrat I und II, Nacht und Träume, Geistertrio (…), Filme für den SDR,* filmedition suhrkamp, Frankfurt am Main 2008; Gaby Hartel, Michael Glasmeier (Hg.), *The Eye of Prey. Beckett's Film-, Fernseh- und Videoarbeiten,* edition suhrkamp, Berlin 2011.

Material Existentialism

Reading over this text on *The American Series* by Oskar Schmidt, certain terms and concepts emerge as characteristic: after-image / facsimile, stage, long exposure, a model quality, the dramaturgy of objects, elimination of people, light and shade, presentation, sparseness, and a poetry of minimal variations. It is, therefore, no great stretch to link Schmidt's photography with the prose and with the drama of Samuel Beckett—and, above all, the films he created in Stuttgart. Beckett's extraordinarily radical films from the 1960s partake of a characteristic that would come to be shared by all his television productions: the figures' movement and speech are confined, as it were, within the gray rectangle of the "playing field," which is echoed by the television format. Basic geometrical shapes—circular and square fields of light, the corners of spaces and openings into spaces, doors and windows opening into blackness and darkness, figures moving on square or on diagonal tracks—give structure and rhythm to minimized and fragmentary plots.[13] Beckett cultivates a dramaturgy of objects and of light, of sparseness; he deploys light in place of darkness and darkness in place of light, with a few accessories placed on the empty stage to formulate a material existentialism, which represses the individuals, relocating them to the imagination. While Beckett may not have been, like Evans, a direct inspiration for Oskar Schmidt, Beckett does place Evans's photography in a different and more essential light.

1 Sherrie Levine, in: *Mannerism: A Theory of Culture,* Vancouver Art Gallery 1982, p. 48.

2 Rosalind Krauss, "The Originality of the Avant-Garde," in: *October* (Cambridge, MA), 18, Fall 1981, pp. 47–66. Quoted from Charles Harrison, Paul Wood, Art in Theory 1900–1990: An Anthology of Changing Ideas, Oxford 1992, p. 1060.

3 See "The Pictures Generation, 1974–1984," exh. cat. The Metropolitan Museum of Art, New York 2009.

4 When one thinks about how the series of the reduced photographic still lifes of Oskar Schmidt were to be located in the field of contemporary art, one must initially remember his early training in painting. The tradition of (surreally staged, invented) painting of the old Leipzig School, but also above all the recent development of the so-called New Leipzig School (represented since 2003 by artists like Thilo Baumgärtel, Tim Eitel, and Martin Weischer) that Schmidt had early on consciously left behind with his photo series. In Leipzig the teaching of Timm Rautert was particularly important for Schmidt: Rautert had always dealt with social themes as a photojournalist and as an artist, with the conceptual photo series and his "image analysis" photography in parallel.

The sculptural staging of Schmidt's photos might also bring him in the vicinity of the work of Thomas Demand. He became well known in the 1990s with his works, starting from photos, reproducing 1:1 historical places, spaces, or objects arranged in still life, that are then—omitting details, text, people, etc.—re-photographed, creating history photos, so to speak, that at the same time represent an extreme concentration of memory.

Under the title "Retrofotografie" Andreas Müller-Pohle has recently exhibited around 20 contemporary photographers, who are behind the current trend of "retro as fallback on aesthetics of the the past." See Andreas Müller-Pohle (ed.), "Retrofotografie," in: *European Photographie,* No. 94, Vol. 34, Issue 2, Winter 2013/14. The author traces two aspects here: firstly, the revival of analog photography, as well as historical techniques like camera obscura and instant photography in their connection with digital devices and applications. Secondly, photographers like Hisaji Hara or Alexandra Polina are presented, who restage art historical models like the painting of Balthus or images of Russian revolutionary art.

5 Oskar Schmidt speaking to the author, September 2013.

6 Bettina Gockel, "Dokumentarisch = Amerikanisch? Zu Oskar Schmidts *Fotoserie The American Series,*" in: *Oskar Schmidt – Dust Bowl Years,* exh. cat. Scheublein + BAK, Zurich 2012.

7 On the aesthetic and scenic interventions of Walker Evans see, among others: http://opinionator.blogs.nytimes.com/2009/10/20/the-case-of-the-inappropriate-alarm-clock-part-3/?_php=true&_type=blogs&_r=0.

8 This book appeared under the title Let Us Now Praise Famous Men (first published in German in 1989 as Preisen will ich die großen Männer).

9 See Johanna Burton, "Not the Last Word. Reflections on Sherrie Levine's *After Walker Evans Negative,*" in: *Artforum,* September 2009, pp. 264–271 f.

10 Documentation for all photos by Levine and Oppenheim at http://www.randomradiance.com/2011_01_01_archive.html.

11 Sherrie Levine, in: Harrison / Wood 2003 (see note 3), p. 1346. Original quotation in: *Flash Art,* 129, Summer 1986.

12 See the discussion of the project in Wired Magazine, 2001, http://archive.wired.com/culture/lifestyle/news/2001/05/43902.

13 Samuel Beckett, *Hey Joe, Quadrat I und II, Nacht und Träume, Geister-Trio …, Filme für den SDR* (Frankfurt am Main, 2008); Gaby Hartel, Michael Glasmeier (ed.), *The Eye of Prey. Beckett's Film-, Fernseh- und Video-arbeiten* (Berlin, 2011).

Biografie / Biography

1977
geboren / born in Erlabrunn, lebt und arbeitet / lives and works in Leipzig und / and Berlin
1998–2002
Studium der Malerei und Grafik an der / Studied painting and graphics at Burg Giebichenstein, Hochschule für Kunst und Design Halle (Saale)
2002–2006
Studium der Fotografie an der / Studied photography at the Hochschule für Grafik und Buchkunst Leipzig
2006–2008
Meisterschüler bei / Master class student with Prof. Timm Rautert an der / at the Hochschule für Grafik und Buchkunst Leipzig

Einzelausstellungen / Solo Exhibitions

2013
The American Series (mit / with Dieter Hiesserer), Galerie Clara Maria Sels, Düsseldorf
2012
Dust Bowl Years, Scheublein + BAK, Zürich / Zurich (Kat. / Cat.)
The American Series I–XII, Parrotta Contemporary Art, Stuttgart
The American Series, Villa Schmitz, Berlin
2011
Pulse New York Projects, Metropolitan Pavilion, New York, NY
Appearances in Light, Galerie Clara Maria Sels, Düsseldorf
2010
Revenants, Goethe-Institut, Washington, D.C. (Kat. / Cat.)
Darkness appears in many ways, Parrotta Contemporary Art, Stuttgart
Johannes Rochhausen / Oskar Schmidt (mit / with Johannes Rochhausen), Wohnung / Apartment Tobias Naehring, Leipzig
2009
Wiedergängerinnen, C/O Berlin, Altes Postfuhramt, Berlin (Kat. / Cat.)
Extend, Galerie Kleindienst, Leipzig
Oskar Schmidt (mit / with Park Jun-Ho), Galerie Clara Maria Sels, Düsseldorf
2008
Attitude of Posture (mit / with Christian Brandl), Safia Galeria, Barcelona (Kat. / Cat.)
Madonna, Hafenrand, Hamburg
2006
Elysium (mit Michael Fandel), LFN / Red Stripe Gallery, Leipzig

Gruppenausstellungen (Auswahl) / Group Exhibitions (Selection)

2014
Fotografie: International. Video, Mixed Media, Daimler Art Collection, Stuttgart
Conceptual and Applied III – Surfaces and Pattern, Daimler Contemporary Berlin
The Beautiful Changes, RH Contemporary Art, New York, NY
Poetik des Raumes, Kunstverein Kiss, Kunst im Schloss Untergröningen
BGL #2, BGL Project, Bergisch Gladbach
2013
Marion-Ermer-Preis 2013 – Die Herstellung von Sichtbarkeit, Neues Museum Weimar (Kat. / Cat.)
Crossing Views – Fotografie aus Leipzig, Marburger Kunstverein, Marburg
Pure Record Not Propaganda, Galerie Baer – Raum für aktuelle Kunst, Dresden
Mit den Augen Düsseldorfer Galeristen – Zeitgenössische Fotografie, E.ON, Düsseldorf
2012
Stillstehende Sachen, SØR Rusche Sammlung, Museum Abtei Liesborn
Überall und Nirgends – Werke aus der Sammlung Reydan Weiss, Villa Jauss, Oberstdorf (Kat. / Cat.)
Room Service, Galerie Kleindienst, Leipzig
2011
Leipzig. Fotografie seit 1839, Museum der bildenden Künste Leipzig (Kat. / Cat.)
Zabludowicz Collection – Recent Photography from Leipzig, Zabludowicz Collection, New York, NY
Hotspot Berlin, Georg-Kolbe-Museum, Berlin (Kat. / Cat.), NY
863 Km + Underworld by Galerie Utopia / The Forgotten Bar Project, Scheublein + BAK, Zürich / Zurich
2010
Art Collection Deutsche Börse – Talents 2009, Deutsche Börse AG, Frankfurt am Main
The Library of Babel, Zabludowicz Collection, London (Kat. / Cat.)
heiter bis wolkig – Positionen aus Leipzig, Berlin und München, Galerie der Künstler, München
17. Leipziger Jahresausstellung, Joseph-Konsum, Leipzig (Kat. / Cat.)
2009
Hab und Gut, Kunsthalle Rostock
Close the Gap – Meisterklasse Timm Rautert, Werkschauhalle Leipziger Baumwollspinnerei, Leipzig; Neuer Pfaffenhofener Kunstverein, Pfaffenhofen; Städtische Galerie, Speyer (Kat. / Cat.)
Stoffe der Eitelkeit, Parrotta Contemporary Art, Stuttgart
Edition Naehring #1, Galerie für Zeitgenössische Kunst, Leipzig
2008
Wir sind nicht hier um uns nett zu finden, Galerie Löhrl, Mönchengladbach (Kat. / Cat.)
Neues Wetter, Universal Cube, Leipzig
Drawcula, Galerie Kleindienst, Leipzig
Close the Gap – Meisterklasse Timm Rautert, Stadtgalerie Kiel; UBS Bank Zürich / Zurich; UBS Wolfsberg (Kat. / Cat.)

Die Freuden der Jugend, Galerie Junges Forum, Wiesbaden
Vertrautes Terrain – Schauraum 1 / Leipziger Schule, Städtische Galerie, Karlsruhe (Kat. / Cat.)
2007
ohne Schatten, Galerie EIGEN + ART, Leipzig
F / Stop – 1. Internationales Fotografiefestival Leipzig, Leipzig (Kat. / Cat.)
Wasser! Fort! Au! Hilfe! Schön! Nicht!, Bieberhaus Hachmannplatz, Hamburg
Mein Katalog und Ich, Galerie Kleindienst, Leipzig (Kat. / Cat.)
2006
bitten. danken. fluchen. grüßen. beten., Ehemalige Privatsynagoge der Jüdischen Mädchenschule, Berlin
Me and My Mirror, Pierogi Gallery New York / Leipzig, Leipzig
the roof, Galerie Kleindienst, Leipzig (Kat. / Cat.)
New Photography from Leipzig, Archeus, London
Artists from Leipzig, Arario Gallery, Peking / Beijing (Kat. / Cat.)
2005
Muse Heute? Inspirationsquellen aktueller Kunst, Kunsthalle Bremen; Städtische Galerie im Buntentor, Bremen (Kat. / Cat.)
Kalte Herzen, Kunstverein Radolfzell / Villa Bosch, Radolfzell
2004
Kalte Herzen, Kunstbunker Tumulka, München (Kat. / Cat.)
2003
Paradies, Kunstförderpreis der Stadtwerke Halle / Leipzig, Kaufhaus am Markt, Halle (Saale) (Kat. / Cat.)

Preise & Stipendien / Awards & Scholarships

2013
Marion-Ermer-Preis (Kat. / Cat.)
2011
Stipendium des Landes Mecklenburg-Vorpommern / Scholarship from the State of Mecklenburg-Western Pomerania im / at Künstlerhaus Lukas, Ahrenshoop
2009
Förderankauf des / Purchase funding of Kunstfonds Sachsen / Kulturstiftung des Freistaates Sachsen
Talents 2009, C/O Berlin (Kat. / Cat.)
2002
Kunstförderpreis / Art award, Stadtwerke Halle / Leipzig (Kat. / Cat.)

Sammlungen / Collections

Staatliche Kunstsammlungen Dresden, Kunstfonds Sachsen
Zabludowicz Collection, London
Daimler Kunst Sammlung, Stuttgart / Berlin
Sammlung Reydan Weiss, Essen
Sammlung Andra Spallart, Wien / Vienna
SØR Rusche Sammlung Oelde / Berlin
Olbricht Collection, Essen / Berlin
Sammlung Daniela Hinrichs, Hamburg
UBS Art Collection, Zürich / Zurich

Oskar Schmidt dankt allen, die am Zustandekommen dieser Publikation mitgewirkt haben, insbesondere / Oskar Schmidt would like to thank everyone who helped realizing this publication, in particular

Anna.k.o.
Nicole Archibeque
Sonja Bahr
Fabian Bechtle
Pauline Izumi Colin
Maisey Cox
Uta Grosenick
Matthias Harder
Sammlung Daniela Hinrichs, Hamburg
William E. Jones
Maria Magdalena Koehn
Christin Krause
Frederik Kugler
Edgar Lecijewski
Michael Mandiberg
Tobias Naehring
Lisa Oppenheim
Galerie Parrotta Contemporary Art, Stuttgart
Timm Rautert
Angelika Richter
Leigh Ruple
Thilo Scheffler
Galerie Scheublein + BAK, Zürich / Zurich
Christian Schmidt
Louis Schmidt
Moritz Schmidt
Veronika Schuster
Galerie Clara Maria Sels, Düsseldorf
Uwe Walter
Renate Wiehager

Gefördert durch die / Supported by
Daimler Art Collection, Stuttgart/Berlin

Herausgeber / Editor: Matthias Harder
Konzeption / Concept: Maria Magdalena Koehn, Oskar Schmidt
Gestaltung / Design: Maria Magdalena Koehn
Texte / Texts: Matthias Harder, Renate Wiehager
Übersetzungen / Translations: Alison Kirkland, Thea Miklowski (S. / pp. 80–92),
Thea Miklowski (S. / pp. 72–76)
Lektorat / Copy Editing: DISTANZ Verlag, Frederik Kugler
Lithografie / Image Editing: anna.k.o. + Uwe Walter, Berlin
Produktion / Production Management: DISTANZ Verlag, Sonja Bahr
Gesamtherstellung / Production: optimal media GmbH, Röbel / Müritz

Umschlag / Cover: *Picture,* 2013, Detail, Archival Inkjet Print, 62,5 × 51 cm

Vertrieb / Distribution
Gestalten, Berlin
www.gestalten.com
sales@gestalten.com

ISBN 978-3-95476-081-7
Printed in Germany

Erschienen im / Published by
DISTANZ Verlag
www.distanz.de